2002

WHAT IS A HATE CRIME?

Other Books in the At Issue Series:

WHAT IS A HATE CRIME?

Roman Espejo, *Book Editor*

Daniel Leone, *Publisher*
Bonnie Szumski, *Editorial Director*
Scott Barbour, *Managing Editor*

An Opposing Viewpoints® Series

Greenhaven Press, Inc.
San Diego, California

Library of Congress Cataloging-in-Publication Data

What is a hate crime? / Roman Espejo, book editor.
     p. cm. — (At issue)
   Includes bibliographical references and index.
   ISBN 0-7377-0812-3 (pbk. : alk. paper) —
ISBN 0-7377-0813-1 (lib. : alk. paper)
   1. Hate crimes. I. Espejo, Roman, 1977– II. Series. III. At issue
(San Diego, Calif.)

HV6773.5 .W48   2002
364.1—dc21   2001023817
                                              CIP

Table of Contents

Introduction

On the night of February 19, 1999, in Sylacuaga, Alabama, Steve Mullins asked his friend Charles Butler to help him kill an acquaintance named Billy Jack Gaither. Butler agreed and watched Mullins beat Gaither with an ax handle and burn his body on top of a pile of tires. Shortly after the crime, they turned themselves into the police and admitted to the killing. Both men were convicted of capital murder and received life in prison without the possibility of parole. Although Mullins, a neo-Nazi skinhead, killed Gaither "'cause he was a faggot," the murder did not make the FBI hate crimes report. Alabama's hate crimes law does not apply to crimes motivated by the victim's sexual orientation.

The brutal, anti-gay murders of Gaither and college student Matthew Shepard, who was killed in Wyoming in 1998, provoked a serious reexamination of existing hate crimes law. The current federal hate crimes statute permits federal prosecution of a hate crime only if the crime was motivated by race, color, national origin, or religion. In addition, the offender must have attempted to hinder the victim's participation in one of six federally protected rights, such as voting or attending a public school. The Hate Crimes Prevention Act (HCPA) was introduced in 1998, 1999, and again in 2000 in an attempt to enhance the present statute. Under the HCPA, hate crimes in which death or bodily injury occurred or a firearm or explosive device was used would be subject to federal investigation, whether or not the victim was participating in a federally protected activity. More importantly, the bill would allow crimes based on sexual orientation, gender, or disability to be investigated by federal authorities. Former President Bill Clinton strongly supported the bill, claiming that it would "strengthen and expand the ability of the Justice System by removing needless jurisdiction requirements." Despite winning the favor of the Senate, the 106th Congress disbanded in 2000 without passing the HCPA.

Though the HCPA has failed to pass a number of times, its supporters have not been discouraged. In 2000, over 100 civil rights, human rights, women's rights, religious, and law enforcement groups launched a web-based campaign promoting the passage of the HCPA called "United Against Hate." Oregon Senator Gordon Smith states, "It has been more than 26 years since the enactment of the Civil Rights Act of 1964, yet countless Americans still encounter discrimination." He planned to introduce the bill to the 107th Congress in 2001.

What is a hate crime?

Americans originally used the term "hate crime" to describe a violent act committed against a person, property, or organization because of actual or perceived differences in race, color, national origin, or religion. The phrase gained popularity as crimes motivated by prejudice and racism received national attention in the 1980s. According to the U.S. Bureau of Justice Assistance, violence against minorities is called "xenophobic" or "right-wing" violence in Germany, where neo-Nazi activity is scrutinized. It is called "racial violence" in nearby Great Britain and France. Hate crimes have also occurred throughout history, from the Romans' religious persecution of Christians to the Hutus' genocidal war against the Tutsis in Rwanda in the 1990s.

Today, the term "hate crime" is used to describe violent incidents in which the perpetrators are not only motivated by differences in race, color, or religion, but by characteristics such as sexual orientation, gender, or disability. For example, when nearly 60 women were sexually and physically assaulted in Central Park in the summer of 1999, many Americans considered the attacks gender-based crimes. Also, the state of Oregon has laws that prohibit discrimination stemming from a myriad of characteristics, from political affiliation to marital status.

Although "hate crime" entered the political lexicon recently, enacting hate crime legislation has been a goal for many lawmakers and activists since the passage of the Civil Rights Act of 1964. In 1968, Congress passed the first law ever to prohibit violence attempting to prevent a person to participate in a federally protected activity because of their race, color, national origin, or religion. In 1981, the Anti-Defamation League released its model of hate crimes legislation, which included the prosecution of hate crimes based on sexual orientation. Forty states and the District of Colombia adopted similar laws thereafter. And in 1990, former President George Bush approved the Hate Crimes Statistics Act, which requires the FBI to compile statistics on all reported hate crimes. The latest enhancement to hate crime legislation was added in 1994, when the Hate Crimes Sentencing Enhancement Act was passed. Under this bill, offenders convicted of hate crimes may be given steeper fines and longer sentences than they would if their actions were not motivated by prejudice.

Equal rights or special treatment?

The most controversial feature of the HCPA is that it attempts to "bring uniformity to the categories covered under current federal hate crimes law" by adding offenses motivated by sexual orientation, gender, and disability to the existing statute, which already prohibits crime based on race, color, national origin, and religion. Its supporters contend that crimes motivated by sexual orientation, gender, or disability deserve federal jurisdiction because they are fundamentally similar to other hate crimes. In the words of Mark Bargerter, "It makes no sense that the FBI can investigate, for example, a religious-based crime, but not a hate crime committed because someone is, or seems to be, gay." Bargerter, a heterosexual man, was brutally beaten and partially blinded by an assailant who presumed he was a homosexual. Advocates of the HCPA also assert that gender should be added to hate crime legislation because victims have been targeted simply because they were women. For example, in 1989, at the University of Montreal, a man wielding a firearm verbally debased feminists and opened fire on female students, killing fourteen of them. Because they are intended to send threatening messages to certain groups, proponents maintain that hate crimes must be swiftly and harshly punished. According to Brian Levin, director of the Center on Hate and Extremism, such crimes "often inspire copycat crimes and a cycle of retaliatory violence by would-be vigilantes."

Critics of hate crimes laws maintain that the criminal justice system deals with hate crimes fairly enough and that the HCPA is not needed. Criminal law professor William J. Stuntz says he does "not see significant social benefits of the bill. It fills no gap in the criminal law." Other opponents claim that including sexual orientation, women, and disability in hate crimes law would create a special class of victims. Some argue that homosexuals, who strongly support the HCPA, seek minority status although they are not, like African Americans, historical victims of oppression. Law professor Lawrence Alexander agrees: "Violence against gays and the disabled, for example, is not a badge or incident of slavery." Detractors also believe that the passage of the HCPA will balkanize the nation by giving select groups special treatment with protective federal laws. "Americans are not equal under the law," argues columnist Heather Brick, "if crimes against a particular 'victim' group are punished more harshly than identical crimes against someone who is not a member of a government-protected group."

The debate over whether or not violence against gays and lesbians, women, and the disabled deserves federal protection has renewed arguments about a much deeper question—whether civil rights laws and the First Amendment protect all Americans equally. *At Issue: What Is a Hate Crime?* presents a wide range of views on the definition of crimes motivated by hatred of those who differ from the majority—a topic of special interest in a nation as diverse as the United States.

1

Hate Crimes Are a Serious Problem

American Psychological Association

The American Psychological Association (APA) is a professional orga-
nization of psychologists that provides mental health information to
mental health care practitioners, researchers, families, and students.

A hate crime is a violent act committed against a person or group
motivated by differences in race, color, national origin, religion,
sexual orientation, gender, or disability. Hate crimes are a serious
problem because they send a threatening message to a certain
group and are more traumatic than other crimes. In recent years,
racially motivated offenses against various ethnic groups have increased, and discriminatory violence against gays and lesbians,
women, and the disabled is often tolerated. However, most hate
crimes are not committed by members of extremist groups, but by
young people acting impulsively upon their personal prejudices.
Therefore, many of these crimes can be prevented. The biases and
stereotypes that encourage hate crimes must be confronted, especially in the nation's education system.

H ate crimes—violent acts against people, property, or organizations because of the group to which they belong or identify with—are a tragic
part of American history. However, it wasn't until early in the 1990s that
the federal government began to collect data on how many and what
kind of hate crimes are being committed, and by whom. Thus, the statis-
tical history on hate crimes is meager. Psychological studies are also fairly
new. Nevertheless, scientific research is beginning to yield some good
perspectives on the general nature of crimes committed because of real or
perceived differences in race, religion, ethnicity or national origin, sexual
orientation, disability, or gender.

According to the FBI, about 30% of hate crimes in 1996, the most recent year for which figures are available, were crimes against property.
They involved robbing, vandalizing, destroying, stealing, or setting fire to
vehicles, homes, stores, or places of worship.

About 70% involve an attack against a person. The offense can range from simple assault (i.e., no weapon is involved) to aggravated assault, rape, and murder. This kind of attack takes place on two levels; not only is it an attack on one's physical self, but it is also an attack on one's very identity.

Who commits hate crimes?

Many people perceive hate crime perpetrators as crazed, hate-filled neo-Nazis or "skinheads". But research by Dr. Edward Dunbar, a clinical psychologist at the University of California, Los Angeles, reveals that of 1,459 hate crimes committed in the Los Angeles area in the period 1994 to 1995, fewer than 5% of the offenders were members of organized hate groups.

Most hate crimes are carried out by otherwise law-abiding young people who see little wrong with their actions. Alcohol and drugs sometimes help fuel these crimes, but the main determinant appears to be personal prejudice, a situation that colors people's judgment, blinding the aggressors to the immorality of what they are doing. Such prejudice is most likely rooted in an environment that disdains someone who is "different" or sees that difference as threatening. One expression of this prejudice is the perception that society sanctions attacks on certain groups. For example, Dr. Karen Franklin, a forensic psychology fellow at the Washington Institute for Mental Illness Research and Training, has found that, in some settings, offenders perceive that they have societal permission to engage in violence against homosexuals.

How much hate crime is out there?

Researchers have concluded that hate crimes are not necessarily random, uncontrollable, or inevitable occurrences. There is overwhelming evidence that society can intervene to reduce or prevent many forms of violence, especially among young people, including the hate-induced violence that threatens and intimidates entire categories of people.

Educated "guesstimates" of the prevalence of hate crimes are difficult because of state-by-state differences in the way such crimes are defined and reported. Federal law enforcement officials have only been compiling nationwide hate crime statistics since 1991, the year after the Hate Crimes Statistics Act was enacted. Before passage of the act, hate crimes were lumped together with such offenses as homicide, assault, rape, robbery, and arson.

In 1996, law enforcement agencies in 49 states and the District of Columbia reported 8,759 bias-motivated criminal offenses to the Federal Bureau of Investigation, the federal government agency mandated by Congress to gather the statistics. However, points out the FBI, these data must be approached with caution. Typically, data on hate crimes collected by social scientists and such groups as the Anti-Defamation League, the National Asian Pacific American Legal Consortium, and the National Gay and Lesbian Task Force show a higher prevalence of hate crime than do federal statistics.

As with most other offenses, reporting hate crimes is voluntary on the part of the local jurisdictions. Some states started submitting data only recently, and not all jurisdictions within states are represented in their reports.

In addition, time frames for reporting are uneven, ranging from one month to an entire year, depending on the jurisdiction. In 1996, only 16% of law enforcement agencies reported any hate crimes in their regions. Eighty-four percent of participating jurisdictions—including states with well-documented histories of racial prejudice—reported zero hate crimes.

Another obstacle to gaining an accurate count of hate crimes is the reluctance of many victims to report such attacks. In fact, they are much less likely than other victims to report crimes to the police, despite—or perhaps because of—the fact that they can frequently identify the perpetrators. This reluctance often derives from the trauma the victim experiences, as well as a fear of retaliation.

Research has concluded that hate crimes are not necessarily random, uncontrollable, or inevitable occurrences.

In a study of gay men and lesbians by Dr. Gregory M. Herek, a psychologist at the University of California, Davis, and his colleagues, Drs. Jeanine Cogan and Roy Gillis, about one-third of the hate crime victims reported the incident to law enforcement authorities, compared with two-thirds of gay and lesbian victims of nonbias crimes. Dr. Dunbar, who studies hate crime in Los Angeles County, has found that victims of severe hate acts (e.g., aggravated and sexual assaults) are the least likely of all hate-crime victims to notify law enforcement agencies, often out of fear of future contact with the perpetrators.

It also appears that some people do not report hate crimes because of fear that the criminal justice system is biased against the group to which the victim belongs and, consequently, that law enforcement authorities will not be responsive. The National Council of La Raza holds that Hispanics often do not report hate crimes because of mistrust of the police.

Another reason for the underreporting of hate crimes is the difficulty of identifying an incident as having been provoked by bias.

Intense feelings of vulnerability, anger, and depression, physical ailments and learning problems, and difficult interpersonal relations—all symptoms of posttraumatic stress disorder—can be brought on by a hate crime.

Dr. Herek and his colleagues found that some hate crime victims have needed as much as 5 years to overcome their ordeal. By contrast, victims of nonbias crimes experienced a decrease in crime-related psychological problems within 2 years of the crime. Like other victims of posttraumatic stress, hate crime victims may heal more quickly when appropriate support and resources are made available soon after the incident occurs.

Hate crimes are message crimes, according to Dr. Jack McDevitt, a criminologist at Northeastern University in Boston. They are different from other crimes in that the offender is sending a message to members of a certain group that they are unwelcome in a particular neighborhood, community, school, or workplace.

Racial hatred and religious discrimination

By far the largest determinant of hate crimes is racial bias, with African Americans the group at greatest risk. In 1996, 4,831 out of the 7,947 such crimes reported to the FBI, or 60%, were promulgated because of race, with close to two-thirds (62%) targeting African Americans. Furthermore, the type of crime committed against this group has not changed much since the 19th century; it still includes bombing and vandalizing churches, burning crosses on home lawns, and murder.

Among the other racially motivated crimes, about 25% were committed against white people, 7% against Asian Pacific Americans, slightly less than 5% against multiracial groups, and 1% against Native Americans and Alaskan Natives.

Ethnic minorities in the United States often become targets of hate crimes because they are perceived to be new to the country even if their families have been here for generations, or simply because they are seen as different from the mainstream population. In the first case, ethnic minorities can fall victim to anti-immigrant bias that includes a recurrent preoccupation with "nativism" (i.e., policies favoring people born in the United States), resentment when so-called "immigrants" succeed (often related to a fear of losing jobs to newcomers), and disdain or anger when they act against the established norm. In the second case, negative stereotypes of certain ethnic groups or people of a certain nationality can fuel antagonism.

Some people do not report hate crimes because of fear that the criminal justice system is biased against the group to which the victim belongs.

Hispanics. People from Latin America are increasingly targets of bias-motivated crimes. Of 814 hate crimes in 1995 motivated by bias based on ethnicity or national origin, the FBI found that 63.3% (or 516) were directed against Hispanics, often because of their immigration status.

Attacks on Hispanics have a particularly long history in California and throughout the Southwest where, during recurring periods of strong anti-immigrant sentiment, both new immigrants and long-time U.S. citizens of Mexican descent were blamed for social and economic problems and harassed or deported en masse.

Asian Pacific Americans. Bias against Asian Pacific Americans, which is increasing today, is long-standing. The Chinese Exclusion Act passed in 1882 barred Chinese laborers from entering this country. Along with trepidation that these workers would take jobs away was the feeling expressed by one Senator during the Congressional debate and reported in *Chronicles of the 20th Century,* that members of this group "do not harmonize with us." The act was not repealed until 1943. Moreover, although the act specifically referred to the Chinese, Japanese people were also affected because most people could not tell the two groups apart. To this day, according to the Leadership Conference on Civil Rights, hostility against one Asian Pacific American group can spill over onto another.

According to the National Asian Pacific American Legal Consortium, 461 anti-Asian incidents were reported in 1995, 2% more than in 1994 and 38% more than in 1993. Moreover, the violence of the incidents increased dramatically; aggravated assaults rose by 14%, and two murders and one firebombing took place. The Leadership Conference on Civil Rights and other experts in the field find that present-day resentment is frequently fueled by the stereotype that Asian Pacific Americans are harder-working, more successful academically, and more affluent than most other Americans.

Arab Americans. Another growing immigrant group experiencing an upsurge in hate crime, largely as a result of Middle East crises, are people of Arab descent. Often they are blamed for incidents to which they have no connection. Thus, at least 227 Muslims were victims of harassment in the period immediately following the bombing of the Murrah federal building in Oklahoma City; an Iraqi refugee in her mid-20s miscarried her near-term baby after an attack on her home in which unknown assailants screaming anti-Islamic epithets broke the windows and pounded on her door, reports the Leadership Conference on Civil Rights.

Most religiously motivated hate crimes are acts of vandalism, although personal attacks are not uncommon. The overwhelming majority (82% in 1996) are directed against Jews, states the FBI. The 781 acts of vandalism that year represent a 7% increase from 1995. However, acts of harassment, threat, or assault went down by 15%, to 941, from a total of 1,116, a decline that the Anti-Defamation League attributes to stronger enforcement of the law and heightened educational outreach.

Bias against Jews has long persisted in the United States. Members of this religious group have been barred (frequently along with black people and Catholics) from attending certain schools, entering certain professions, holding certain jobs, or moving into certain neighborhoods. Although these abrogations of civil rights are now illegal, conspiracy theories about Jewish involvement in international cabals and Jewish exploitation of African Americans still make the rounds today.

Most of the property crimes involve vandalism. In 1997, for example, SS lightning bolts and swastikas were among the anti-Semitic graffiti discovered in Hebrew and Yiddish books in the University of Chicago library, and an explosive device was detonated at the door of a Jewish center in New York City. But personal assaults against Jews are not uncommon. That same year, two men with a BB gun entered a Wisconsin synagogue and started shooting during morning prayers. In 1995 in Cincinnati, a gang member revealed that one of the victims of his group's initiation ceremony was chosen just because he was Jewish.

Gender-based bias and disdain of gays and lesbians

Gender-based violence is a significant social and historical problem, with women the predominant victims. Only recently, however, have these acts of violence been characterized as hate crimes. The Hate Crimes Prevention Act of 1998 would make gender a category of bias-motivated crime. [It didn't pass.]

Except for crimes against homosexuals, the federal Hate Crimes Statistics Act does not collect data on gender. However, a recent national survey found that 7.2 of every 1,000 women each year are victims of rape. In testimony for a Congressional hearing on domestic violence, University of Maryland psychology professor Dr. Lisa Goodman reported that two decades of research indicate that at least two million women in the United States may be the victims of severe assaults by their male partners in an average 12-month period. At least 21% of all women are physically assaulted by an intimate male at least once during adulthood. More than half of all women (52%) murdered in the United States in the first half of the 1980s were killed by their partners.

The more violence a woman experiences, the more she suffers from psychological distress that spills over into many areas of life. Most violence against women is not committed during random encounters but by a current or former male partner. Exposed to attacks and threats over and over again, victims often live with increasing levels of isolation and terror. Typical long-term effects of male violence in an intimate adult relationship are low self-esteem, depression, and posttraumatic stress disorder. These problems are compounded by psychophysiological complaints such as gastrointestinal problems, severe headaches, and insomnia.

The most socially acceptable, and probably the most widespread, form of hate crime among teenagers and young adults are those targeting sexual minorities, says Dr. Franklin. She has identified four categories of assaulters involved in such crimes, as follows:

- Ideology assailants report that their crimes stem from their negative beliefs and attitudes about homosexuality that they perceive other people in the community share. They see themselves as enforcing social morals.
- Thrill seekers are typically adolescents who commit assaults to alleviate boredom, to have fun and excitement, and to feel strong.
- Peer-dynamics assailants also tend to be adolescents; they commit assaults in an effort to prove their toughness and heterosexuality to friends.
- Self-defense assailants typically believe that homosexuals are sexual predators and say they were responding to aggressive sexual propositions.

Of nearly 2,000 gay and lesbian people surveyed in Sacramento, California, by Dr. Herek, roughly one-fifth of the women and one-fourth of the men reported being the victim of a hate crime since age 16. One woman in eight and one man in six had been victimized within the last 5 years. More than half the respondents reported antigay verbal threats and harassment in the year before the survey.

Scorn of people with disabilities

Congress amended the Hate Crimes Statistics Act in 1994 to add disabilities as a category for which hate crimes data are to be collected. Because the FBI only began collecting statistics on disability bias in 1997, results are not yet available. However, we know from social science research that the pervasive stigma that people apply to both mental and physical disability is expressed in many forms of discriminatory behaviors and practices, including increased risk for sexual and physical abuse.

The Judge David L. Bazelon Center for Mental Health Law, a national organization representing low-income adults and children with mental disabilities, holds that such hate crimes are motivated by the perception that people with disabilities are not equal, deserving, contributing members of society, and, therefore, it is okay to attack them.

Although racial and ethnic tensions are thought to increase during economic downswings, Dr. Donald P. Green, a political scientist at Yale University, has found that a weak economy does not necessarily result in an increase in hate crimes. His analysis of past incidents shows scant evidence that lynchings of black people in the pre-Depression South increased in response to downturns in cotton prices or general economic conditions. Monthly hate crime statistics gathered by the Bias Crime Unit of the New York City Police Department show similar results: High unemployment does not give rise to hate crimes "regardless of whether we speak of black, Latino, Jewish, Asian, gay and lesbian, or white victims," according to Green.

High unemployment does not give rise to hate crimes "regardless of whether we speak of black, Latino, Jewish, Asian, gay and lesbian, or white victims."

However, one form of economic change that may set the stage for racist hate crimes occurs when minorities first move into an ethnically homogeneous area. According to Dr. Green, the resulting violent reaction seems to be based on a visceral aversion to social change. The offenders frequently justify the use of force to preserve what they see as their disappearing, traditional way of life. The more rapid the change, holds Dr. Green, the more likely violence will occur.

The 1980s, for example, witnessed the rapid disappearance of homogeneous white enclaves within large cities, with an attendant surge in urban hate crimes. A classic example is the Canarsie neighborhood in Brooklyn, which was primarily white until large numbers of nonwhites arrived. The influx led to a rash of hate crimes.

Conversely, says Dr. Green, integrated neighborhoods, sometimes characterized as cauldrons of racial hostility, tend to have lower rates of hate crime than neighborhoods on the verge of integration.

Is there anything we can do?

Because of insufficient information on the extent of hate crimes, it is likely that many law enforcement agencies and communities are not taking the necessary steps to stamp out these violations of law and order. It is also likely that only a small percentage of hate crime victims receive the medical and mental health services that public and nonprofit agencies make available to victims of violent crime; thus, their pain and suffering is more likely to become a heavy burden and last many years longer than is typical for other crime victims.

The American Psychological Association, therefore, has urged that Congress undertake the following actions:

- Support federal antidiscrimination laws, statutes, and regulations that ensure full legal protection against discrimination and hate-motivated violence. Most important, enact the Hate Crimes Prevention Act of 1998.

- Increase support of the Community Relations Service (CRS), an arm of the Department of Justice that works with local officials to resolve racial and ethnic conflicts and is often seen as the federal government's peacemaker.
- Support programs that offer training for police and victim-assistance professionals on early intervention techniques that help hate crime victims better cope with trauma. The curriculum could be similar to one developed by the CRS.
- Encourage communities to launch educational efforts aimed at dispelling minority stereotypes, reducing hostility between groups, and encouraging broader intercultural understanding and appreciation. Specifically, according to Dr. Franklin, it is important that school administrators, school boards, and classroom teachers constantly confront harassment and denigration of those who are different. Antibias teaching should start in early childhood and continue through high school. Teachers must also know that they have the backing of administrators and school board members to intervene against incidents of bias whether inside the school or on the playground.

2

Whites Are Victims of Hate Crimes

Clarence Page

Clarence Page is a nationally syndicated columnist and member of the editorial staff of the Chicago Tribune. *He won the 1987 American Civil Liberties Union James P. McGuire Award for his columns on constitutional rights and a 1989 Pulitzer Prize for commentary.*

A common misperception is that only whites are guilty, yet whites are never victims, of race crimes. While most high profile hate crimes involve violence committed by whites against ethnic minorities, race crimes against whites generally go unnoticed. Also, hate crimes perpetuated by and against whites are often inaccurately reported. For instance, in the FBI's annual hate crime reports, a Hispanic victim is counted as a minority while a Hispanic offender is counted as "white." If hate-crime laws were applied equally to whites and nonwhites, opposition to such laws would diminish.

Is there an undercount of white hate-crime victims? It is easy to be skeptical about that charge. After all, it tends to be voiced most often and loudly by those who never wanted hate-crime laws to be passed in the first place.

Nevertheless, I, for one, take the charge seriously. As an African American, one of the groups that hate-crime laws were written to protect, I have a vested interest in making sure everyone, including white people, is equally protected by them.

No group has a monopoly on hate, nor is anyone immune to it. If not everyone feels they get a fair shake from such laws, which are designed to enhance penalties for crimes that are hate-motivated, only the haters win.

Unfortunately, a cursory look at recent high-profile hate-crime cases fuels the suspicions of the skeptics like Louis Calabro, a retired San Francisco police lieutenant who now lives in San Bruno, Calif. He was so concerned about bias against his fellow whites, whom he prefers to call "European Americans," that he founded the European/American Issues Forum.

No, as humor columnist Dave Barry likes to say, I am not making this up.

Mr. Calabro did not want to discuss in a telephone interview with me how many members are in his group, which was born on the heels of the fight over anti-affirmative action Proposition 209. Nevertheless, he has raised some thought-provoking points in his recent letter-writing campaign to the White House and Congress, including whether there may be an undercount of white victims and an overcount of white hate-crime perpetrators.

For example, the FBI's annual hate-crime reports list "Hispanics" as a victim category, but not as a perpetrator category. As a result, Mr. Calabro points out, "A Hispanic victim is counted as Hispanic, but a Hispanic perpetrator is counted as white."

Maybe. Or, as I pointed out, a Hispanic perpetrator might wind up being counted as black, if the label fits. "Hispanics" come in all colors. It is hard to be precise about something so imprecise as race and ethnicity in a mulligan-stew nation like the United States.

Nevertheless, Mr. Calabro's complaint led me to think about the biases police, the press and politicians may have about who commits *hate* crimes.

For example, a white immigration lawyer went berserk and killed five people—a Jewish woman, an Indian man, two Asian men and one black man—in a late April shooting spree in Pittsburgh. Police found a typewritten note, and media labeled the killings a possible "hate crime" within 24 hours.

But media and police seemed much less eager to attach the "hate crime" label to a similar killing spree two months earlier by a black man, Ronald Taylor, who shot five whites, killing three, in the Pittsburgh suburbs. Police found "hate writings" in Taylor's apartment that were aimed at Jews, Asians, Italians and "the media," news reports said, but they omitted the term "hate crime" from most reports. I had to call the county prosecutor's office to confirm that, indeed, Taylor had been charged under Pennsylvania's version of laws that enhance penalties for hate-motivated crimes.

No group has a monopoly on hate, nor is anyone immune to it.

Talk shows and Web sites have been buzzing more recently regarding the fatal stabbing of a white 8-year-old, Kevin Shifflett, by a black man, while the boy was playing in front of his great-grandparents' home in Alexandria, Va., in April.

Witnesses said the man made comments about killing white people during the attack. A note was later found with the phrase "Kill them racist white kids" in broken and misspelled English in a hotel room where the prime suspect had stayed.

Yet, more than a week after the note was found, authorities were reluctant to call the crime a hate crime, even in media interviews.

Suspicions were further inflamed when the *Washington Times* reported last week that investigators had withheld racially sensitive information from their fellow officers, as well as the public.

How come? Given how hypersensitive issues of race and ethnicity can be, I am not quick to fault officials who want to downplay the issue when it is not germane. But, with hate crimes, it is the whole point of the law.

Suppressing the race angle may cool tensions for a while, but ultimately it can heighten stereotypes that hate crimes are for whites to commit and other crimes (unhateful crimes?) are for everyone else.

Opponents of hate crimes may not have found their smoking gun. But they have found enough smoke to make a reasonable observer wonder whether there might be a fire somewhere.

Significantly, the 1993 case under which the Supreme Court first upheld hate-crime laws was a Milwaukee case involving black defendants who had attacked a white 14-year-old boy. Nevertheless, the myth persists that the laws were directed against whites to protect minorities.

The sooner we eradicate that myth, the fewer reasons anyone but the haters will have for despising hate-crime laws.

3

Hate Crimes Are Not a Serious Problem

Andrew Sullivan

Andrew Sullivan, the former editor of the New Republic, *is a contributing writer to* The New York Times Magazine *and the author of* Virtually Normal.

Hate is a vague, complex, and highly personal emotion and does not pertain to a particular set of beliefs. Thus, labeling violent acts committed against certain victims as "hate crimes" is deeply problematic and possibly unconstitutional. Moreover, "equal opportunity" crimes such as random acts of violence pose a bigger threat to society. They occur much more frequently than hate crimes, are no less brutal, and threaten the safety of entire communities, not just particular groups. Violence is a serious problem that must be addressed, but hate is an immutable aspect of a free society that can only be reduced, not eradicated. The concept of hate crimes is harmful at worst, redundant at best, and should be done away with.

I wonder what was going on in John William King's head in 1997 when he tied James Byrd Jr.'s feet to the back of a pickup truck and dragged him three miles down a road in rural Texas. King and two friends had picked up Byrd, who was black, when he was walking home, half-drunk, from a party. As part of a bonding ritual in their fledgling white supremacist group, the three men took Byrd to a remote part of town, beat him and chained his legs together before attaching them to the truck. Pathologists at King's trial testified that Byrd was probably alive and conscious until his body finally hit a culvert and split in two. When King was offered a chance to say something to Byrd's family at the trial, he smirked and uttered an obscenity.

We know all these details now, many months later. We know quite a large amount about what happened before and after. But I am still drawn, again and again, to the flash of ignition, the moment when fear and loathing became hate, the instant of transformation when King became hunter and Byrd became prey.

What was that? And what was it when Buford Furrow Jr., longtime member of the Aryan Nations, calmly walked up to a Filipino-American mailman he happened to spot, asked him to mail a letter and then shot him at point-blank range? Or when Russell Henderson beat Matthew Shepard, a young gay man, to a pulp, removed his shoes and then, with the help of a friend, tied him to a post, like a dead coyote, to warn off others?

For all our documentation of these crimes and others, our political and moral disgust at them, our morbid fascination with them, our sensitivity to their social meaning, we seem at times to have no better idea now than we ever had of what exactly they were about. About what that moment means when, for some reason or other, one human being asserts absolute, immutable superiority over another. About not the violence, but what the violence expresses. About what—exactly—hate is. And what our own part in it may be.

The new offense

I find myself wondering what hate actually is in part because we have created an entirely new offense in American criminal law—a "hate crime"—to combat it. And barely a day goes by without someone somewhere declaring war against it. In August 1999, President Clinton called for an expansion of hate-crime laws as "what America needs in our battle against hate." A couple of weeks later, Senator John McCain used a campaign speech to denounce the "hate" he said poisoned the land. New York's Mayor, Rudolph Giuliani, recently tried to stop the Million Youth March in Harlem on the grounds that the event was organized by people "involved in hate marches and hate rhetoric."

The media concurs in its emphasis. In 1985, there were 11 mentions of "hate crimes" in the national media database Nexis. By 1990, there were more than a thousand. In the first six months of 1999, there were 7,000. "Sexy fun is one thing," wrote a *New York Times* reporter about sexual assaults in Woodstock '99's mosh pit. "But this was an orgy of lewdness tinged with hate." And when Benjamin Smith marked the Fourth of July in 1999 by targeting blacks, Asians and Jews for murder in Indiana and Illinois, the story wasn't merely about a twisted young man who had emerged on the scene. As *The Times* put it, "Hate arrived in the neighborhoods of Indiana University, in Bloomington, in the early-morning darkness."

But what exactly was this thing that arrived in the early-morning darkness? For all our zeal to attack hate, we still have a remarkably vague idea of what it actually is. A single word, after all, tells us less, not more. For all its emotional punch, "hate" is far less nuanced an idea than prejudice, or bigotry, or bias, or anger, or even mere aversion to others. Is it to stand in for all these varieties of human experience—and everything in between? If so, then the war against it will be so vast as to be quixotic. Or is "hate" to stand for a very specific idea or belief, or set of beliefs, with a very specific object or group of objects? Then waging war against it is almost certainly unconstitutional. Perhaps these kinds of questions are of no concern to those waging war on hate. Perhaps it is enough for them that they share a sentiment that there is too much hate and never enough vigilance in combating it. But sentiment is a poor basis for law, and a dangerous tool in politics. It is better to leave some unwinnable wars unfought.

The views of hate

Hate is everywhere. Human beings generalize all the time, ahead of time, about everyone and everything. A large part of it may even be hardwired. At some point in our evolution, being able to know beforehand who was friend or foe was not merely a matter of philosophical reflection. It was a matter of survival. And even today it seems impossible to feel a loyalty without also feeling a disloyalty, a sense of belonging without an equal sense of unbelonging. We're social beings. We associate. Therefore we disassociate. And although it would be comforting to think that the one could happen without the other, we know in reality that it doesn't. How many patriots are there who have never felt a twinge of xenophobia?

Of course by hate, we mean something graver and darker than this kind of lazy prejudice. But the closer you look at this distinction, the fuzzier it gets. Much of the time, we harbor little or no malice toward people of other backgrounds or places or ethnicities or ways of life. But then a car cuts you off at an intersection and you find yourself noticing immediately that the driver is a woman, or black, or old, or fat, or white, or male. Or you are walking down a city street at night and hear footsteps quickening behind you. You look around and see that it is a white woman and not a black man, and you are instantly relieved. These impulses are so spontaneous they are almost involuntary. But where did they come from? The mindless need to be mad at someone—anyone—or the unconscious eruption of a darker prejudice festering within?

For all our zeal to attack hate, we still have a remarkably vague idea of what it actually is.

In 1993, in San Jose, Calif., two neighbors—one heterosexual, one homosexual—were engaged in a protracted squabble over grass clippings. (The full case is recounted in "Hate Crimes," by James B. Jacobs and Kimberly Potter.) The gay man regularly mowed his lawn without a grass catcher, which prompted his neighbor to complain on many occasions that grass clippings spilled over onto his driveway. Tensions grew until one day, the gay man mowed his front yard, spilling clippings onto his neighbor's driveway, prompting the straight man to yell an obscene and common anti-gay insult. The wrangling escalated. At one point, the gay man agreed to collect the clippings from his neighbor's driveway but then later found them dumped on his own porch. A fracas ensued with the gay man spraying the straight man's son with a garden hose, and the son hitting and kicking the gay man several times, yelling anti-gay slurs. The police were called, and the son was eventually convicted of a hate-motivated assault, a felony. But what was the nature of the hate: anti-gay bias, or suburban property-owner madness?

Or take the Labor Day parade in 1998 in Broad Channel, a small island in Jamaica Bay, Queens. Almost everyone there is white, and in recent years a group of local volunteer firefighters has taken to decorating a pickup truck for the parade in order to win the prize for "funniest float." Their themes have tended toward the outrageously provocative. Beginning in 1995, they won prizes for floats depicting "Hasidic Park," "Gooks of Hazzard" and "Happy Gays." In 1998, they called their float "Black to the Future, Broad Channel 2098." They imagined their community a century hence as a largely black enclave, with every stereotype imaginable: watermelons, basketballs and so on. At one point during the parade, one of them mimicked the dragging death of James Byrd. It was caught on videotape, and before long the entire community was depicted as a caldron of hate.

> *The modern words that we have created to describe the varieties of hate—"sexism," "racism," "anti-Semitism," "homophobia". . . tell us merely the identities of the victims.*

It's an interesting case, because the float was indisputably in bad taste and the improvisation on the Byrd killing was grotesque. But was it hate? The men on the float were local heroes for their volunteer work; they had no record of bigoted activity, and were not members of any racist organizations. In previous years, they had made fun of many other groups and saw themselves more as provocateurs than bigots. When they were described as racists, it came as a shock to them. They apologized for poor taste but refused to confess to bigotry. "The people involved aren't horrible people," protested a local woman. "Was it a racist act? I don't know. Are they racists? I don't think so."

If hate is a self-conscious activity, she has a point. The men were primarily motivated by the desire to shock and to reflect what they thought was their community's culture. Their display was not aimed at any particular black people, or at any blacks who lived in Broad Channel—almost none do. But if hate is primarily an unconscious activity, then the matter is obviously murkier. And by taking the horrific lynching of a black man as a spontaneous object of humor, the men were clearly advocating indifference to it. Was this an aberrant excess? Or the real truth about the men's feelings toward African-Americans? Hate or tastelessness? And how on earth is anyone, even perhaps the firefighters themselves, going to know for sure?

Or recall H.L. Mencken. He shared in the anti-Semitism of his time with more alacrity than most and was an indefatigable racist. "It is impossible," he wrote in his diary, "to talk anything resembling discretion or judgment into a colored woman. They are all essentially childlike, and even hard experience does not teach them anything." He wrote at another time of the "psychological stigmata" of the "Afro-American race." But it is also true that, during much of his life, day to day, Mencken conducted himself with no regard to race, and supported a politics that was clearly integrationist. As the editor of his diary has pointed out, Mencken published many black authors in his magazine, the *Mercury*, and lobbied on their behalf with his publisher, Alfred A. Knopf. The last thing Mencken ever wrote was a diatribe against racial segregation in Baltimore's public parks. He was good friends with leading black writers and journalists, including James Weldon Johnson, Walter White and George S. Schuyler, and played an underappreciated role in promoting the Harlem Renaissance.

What would our modern view of hate do with Mencken? Probably ignore him, or change the subject. But, with regard to hate, I know lots of people like Mencken. He reminds me of conservative friends who oppose almost every measure for homosexual equality yet genuinely delight in the company of their gay friends. It would be easier for me to think of them as haters, and on paper, perhaps, there is a good case that they are. But in real life, I know they are not. Some of them clearly harbor no real malice toward me or other homosexuals whatsoever.

They are as hard to figure out as those liberal friends who support every gay rights measure they have ever heard of but do anything to avoid going into a gay bar with me. I have to ask myself in the same, frustrating kind of way: are they liberal bigots or bigoted liberals? Or are they neither bigots nor liberals, but merely people?

The complexities of hate

Hate used to be easier to understand. When Sartre described anti-Semitism in his 1946 essay "Anti-Semite and Jew," he meant a very specific array of firmly held prejudices, with a history, an ideology and even a pseudo-science to back them up. He meant a systematic attempt to demonize and eradicate an entire race. If you go to the Web site of the World Church of the Creator, the organization that inspired young Benjamin Smith to murder in Illinois in 1999, you will find a similarly bizarre, pseudorational ideology. The kind of literature read by Buford Furrow before he rained terror on a Jewish kindergarten and then killed a mailman because of his color is full of the same paranoid loopiness. And when we talk about hate, we often mean this kind of phenomenon.

But this brand of hatred is mercifully rare in the United States. These professional maniacs are to hate what serial killers are to murder. They should certainly not be ignored; but they represent what Harold Meyerson, writing in Salon, called "niche haters": coldblooded, somewhat deranged, often poorly socialized psychopaths. In a free society with relatively easy access to guns, they will always pose a menace.

But their menace is a limited one, and their hatred is hardly typical of anything very widespread. Take Buford Furrow. He famously issued a "wake-up call" to "kill Jews" in Los Angeles, before he peppered a Jewish community center with gunfire. He did this in a state with two Jewish female Senators, in a city with a large, prosperous Jewish population, in a country where out of several million Jewish Americans, a total of 66 were reported by the F.B.I. as the targets of hate-crime assaults in 1997. However despicable Furrow's actions were, it would require a very large stretch to describe them as representative of anything but the deranged fringe of an American subculture.

Most hate is more common and more complicated, with as many varieties as there are varieties of love. Just as there is possessive love and needy love; family love and friendship; romantic love and unrequited love; passion and respect, affection and obsession, so hatred has its shadings. There is hate that fears, and hate that merely feels contempt; there is hate that expresses power, and hate that comes from powerlessness; there is revenge, and there is hate that comes from envy. There is hate that was love, and hate that is a curious expression of love. There is hate of the other, and hate of something that reminds us too much of ourselves. There is the oppressor's hate, and the victim's hate. There is hate that burns slowly, and hate that fades. And there is hate that explodes, and hate that never catches fire.

A purely random murder may be even more terrifying than a targeted one, since the entire community, and not just a part of it, feels threatened.

The modern words that we have created to describe the varieties of hate—"sexism," "racism," "anti-Semitism, "homophobia"—tell us very little about any of this. They tell us merely the identities of the victims; they don't reveal the identities of the perpetrators, or what they think, or how they feel. They don't even tell us how the victims feel. And this simplicity is no accident. Coming from the theories of Marxist and post-Marxist academics, these "isms" are far better at alleging structures of power than at delineating the workings of the individual heart or mind. In fact, these "isms" can exist without mentioning individuals at all.

We speak of institutional racism, for example, as if an institution can feel anything. We talk of "hate" as an impersonal noun, with no hater specified. But when these abstractions are actually incarnated, when someone feels something as a result of them, when a hater actually interacts with a victim, the picture changes. We find that hates are often very different phenomena one from another, that they have very different psychological dynamics, that they might even be better understood by not seeing them as varieties of the same thing at all.

There is, for example, the now unfashionable distinction between reasonable hate and unreasonable hate. In recent years, we have become accustomed to talking about hates as if they were all equally indefensible, as if it could never be the case that some hates might be legitimate, even necessary. But when some 800,000 Tutsis are murdered under the auspices of a Hutu regime in Rwanda, and when a few thousand Hutus are killed in revenge, the hates are not commensurate. Genocide is not an event like a hurricane, in which damage is random and universal; it is a planned and often merciless attack of one group upon another. The hate of the perpetrators is a monstrosity. The hate of the victims, and their survivors, is justified. What else, one wonders, were surviving Jews supposed to feel toward Germans after the Holocaust? Or, to a different degree, South African blacks after apartheid? If the victims overcome this hate, it is a supreme moral achievement. But if they don't, the victims are not as culpable as the perpetrators. So the hatred of Serbs for Kosovars today can never be equated with the hatred of Kosovars for Serbs.

Hate, like much of human feeling, is not rational, but it usually has its reasons. And it cannot be understood, let alone condemned, without knowing them. Similarly, the hate that comes from knowledge is always different from the hate that comes from ignorance. It is one of the most foolish cliches of our time that prejudice is always rooted in ignorance, and can usually be overcome by familiarity with the objects of our loathing. The racism of many Southern whites under segregation was not appeased by familiarity with Southern blacks; the virulent loathing of Tutsis by many Hutus was not undermined by living next door to them for centuries. Theirs was a hatred that sprang, for whatever reasons, from experience. It cannot easily be compared with, for example, the resilience of anti-Semitism in Japan, or hostility to immigration in areas where immigrants are unknown, or fear of homosexuals by people who have never knowingly met one.

The same familiarity is an integral part of what has become known as "sexism." Sexism isn't, properly speaking, a prejudice at all. Few men live without knowledge or constant awareness of women. Every single sexist man was born of a woman, and is likely to be sexually attracted to women. His hostility is going to be very different than that of, say, a reclusive member of the Aryan Nations toward Jews he has never met.

In her book *The Anatomy of Prejudices*, the psychotherapist Elisabeth Young-Bruehl proposes a typology of three distinct kinds of hate: obsessive, hysterical and narcissistic. It's not an exhaustive analysis, but it's a beginning in any serious attempt to understand hate rather than merely declaring war on it. The obsessives, for Young-Bruehl, are those, like the Nazis or Hutus, who fantasize a threat from a minority, and obsessively try to rid themselves of it. For them, the very existence of the hated group is threatening. They often describe their loathing in almost physical terms: they experience what Patrick Buchanan, in reference to homosexuals, once described as a "visceral recoil" from the objects of their detestation. They often describe those they hate as diseased or sick, in need of a cure. Or they talk of "cleansing" them, as the Hutus talked of the Tutsis, or call them "cockroaches," as Yitzhak Shamir called the Palestinians. If you read material from the Family Research Council, it is clear that the group regards homosexuals as similar contaminants. A recent posting on its Web site about syphilis among gay men was headlined, "Unclean."

For if every crime is possibly a hate crime, then it is simply another name for crime.

Hysterical haters have a more complicated relationship with the objects of their aversion. In Young-Bruehl's words, hysterical prejudice is a prejudice that "a person uses unconsciously to appoint a group to act out in the world forbidden sexual and sexually aggressive desires that the person has repressed." Certain kinds of racists fit this pattern. White loathing of blacks is, for some people, at least partly about sexual and physical envy. A certain kind of white racist sees in black America all those impulses he wishes most to express himself but cannot. He idealizes in "blackness" a sexual freedom, a physical power, a Dionysian release that he detests but also longs for. His fantasy may not have any basis in reality, but it is powerful nonetheless. It is a form of love-hate, and it is impossible to understand the nuances of racism in, say, the American South, or in British Imperial India, without it.

Unlike the obsessives, the hysterical haters do not want to eradicate the objects of their loathing; rather they want to keep them in some kind of permanent and safe subjugation in order to indulge the attraction of their repulsion. A recent study, for example, found that the men most likely to be opposed to equal rights for homosexuals were those most likely to be aroused by homoerotic imagery. This makes little rational sense, but it has a certain psychological plausibility. If homosexuals were granted equality, then the hysterical gay-hater might panic that his repressed passions would run out of control, overwhelming him and the world he inhabits.

Murder, which dominates media coverage of hate crimes, is a tiny proportion of the total.

A narcissistic hate, according to Young-Bruehl's definition, is sexism. In its most common form, it is rooted in many men's inability even to imagine what it is to be a woman, a failing rarely challenged by men's control of our most powerful public social institutions. Women are not so much hated by most men as simply ignored in nonsexual contexts, or never conceived of as true equals. The implicit condescension is mixed, in many cases, with repressed and sublimated erotic desire. So the unawareness of women is sometimes commingled with a deep longing or contempt for them.

Each hate, of course, is more complicated than this, and in any one person hate can assume a uniquely configured combination of these types. So there are hysterical sexists who hate women because they need them so much, and narcissistic sexists who hardly notice that women exist, and sexists who oscillate between one of these positions and another. And there are gay-bashers who are threatened by masculine gay men and gay-haters who feel repulsed by effeminate ones. The soldier who beat his fellow soldier Barry Winchell to death with a baseball bat in July 1999 had earlier lost a fight to him. It was the image of a macho gay man—and the shame of being bested by him—that the vengeful soldier had to obliterate, even if he needed a gang of accomplices and a weapon to do so. But the murderers of Matthew Shepard seem to have had a different impulse: a visceral disgust at the thought of any sexual contact with an effeminate homosexual. Their anger was mixed with mockery, as the cruel spectacle at the side of the road suggested.

In the same way, the pathological anti-Semitism of Nazi Germany was obsessive, inasmuch as it tried to cleanse the world of Jews; but also, as Daniel Jonah Goldhagen shows in his book, *Hitler's Willing Executioners*, hysterical. The Germans were mysteriously compelled as well as repelled by Jews, devising elaborate ways, like death camps and death marches, to keep them alive even as they killed them. And the early Nazi phobia of interracial sex suggests as well a lingering erotic quality to the relationship, partaking of exactly the kind of sexual panic that persists among some homosexual-haters and anti-miscegenation racists. So the concept of "homophobia," like that of "sexism" and "racism," is often a crude one. All three are essentially cookie-cutter formulas that try to understand human impulses merely through the one-dimensional identity of the victims, rather than through the thoughts and feelings of the haters and hated.

This is deliberate. The theorists behind these "isms" want to ascribe all blame to one group in society—the "oppressors"—and render specific others—the "victims"—completely blameless. And they want to do this in order in part to side unequivocally with the underdog. But it doesn't take a genius to see how this approach, too, can generate its own form of bias. It can justify blanket condemnations of whole groups of people— white straight males for example—purely because of the color of their skin or the nature of their sexual orientation. And it can condescendingly ascribe innocence to whole groups of others. It does exactly what hate does: it hammers the uniqueness of each individual into the anvil of group identity. And it postures morally over the result.

In reality, human beings and human acts are far more complex, which is why these isms and the laws they have fomented are continually coming under strain and challenge. Once again, hate wriggles free of its definers. It knows no monolithic groups of haters and hated. Like a river, it has many eddies, backwaters and rapids. So there are anti-Semites who actually admire what they think of as Jewish power, and there are gay-haters who look up to homosexuals and some who want to sleep with them. And there are black racists, racist Jews, sexist women and anti-Semitic homosexuals. Of course there are.

Hate-victimizers as hate victims

Once you start thinking of these phenomena less as the "isms" of sexism, racism and "homophobia," once you think of them as independent psychological responses, it's also possible to see how they can work in a bewildering variety of ways in a bewildering number of people. To take one obvious and sad oddity: people who are demeaned and objectified in society may develop an aversion to their tormentors that is more hateful in its expression than the prejudice they have been subjected to. The F.B.I. statistics on hate crimes throws up an interesting point. In America in the 1990's, blacks were up to three times as likely as whites to commit a hate crime, to express their hate by physically attacking their targets or their property. Just as sexual abusers have often been victims of sexual abuse, and wife-beaters often grew up in violent households, so hate criminals may often be members of hated groups.

Even the Columbine murderers were in some sense victims of hate before they were purveyors of it. Their classmates later admitted that Dylan Klebold and Eric Harris were regularly called "faggots" in the corridors and classrooms of Columbine High and that nothing was done to prevent or stop the harassment. This climate of hostility doesn't excuse the actions of Klebold and Harris, but it does provide a more plausible context. If they had been black, had routinely been called "nigger" in the school and had then exploded into a shooting spree against white students, the response to the matter might well have been different. But the hate would have been the same. In other words, hate-victims are often hate-victimizers as well. This doesn't mean that all hates are equivalent, or that some are not more justified than others. It means merely that hate goes both ways; and if you try to regulate it among some, you will find yourself forced to regulate it among others.

It is no secret, for example, that some of the most vicious anti-Semites in America are black, and that some of the most virulent anti-Catholic bigots in America are gay. At what point, we are increasingly forced to ask, do these phenomena become as indefensible as white racism or religious toleration of anti-gay bigotry? That question becomes all the more difficult when we notice that it is often minorities who commit some of the most hate-filled offenses against what they see as their oppressors. It was the mainly gay AIDS activist group Act Up that perpetrated the hateful act of desecrating Communion hosts at a Mass at St Patrick's Cathedral in New York. And here is the playwright Tony Kushner, who is gay, responding to the Matthew Shepard beating in *The Nation* magazine: "Pope John Paul II endorses murder. He, too, knows the price of discrimination, having declared anti-Semitism a sin. . . . He knows that discrimination kills. But when the Pope heard the news about Matthew Shepard, he, too, worried about spin. And so, on the subject of gay-bashing, the Pope and his cardinals and his bishops and priests maintain their cynical political silence. . . . To remain silent is to endorse murder." Kushner went on to describe the Pope as a "homicidal liar."

Maybe the passion behind these words is justified. But it seems clear enough to me that Kushner is expressing hate toward the institution of the Catholic Church, and all those who perpetuate its doctrines. How else to interpret the way in which he accuses the Pope of cynicism, lying and murder? And how else either to understand the brutal parody of religious vocations expressed by the Sisters of Perpetual Indulgence, a group of gay men who dress in drag as nuns and engage in sexually explicit performances in public? Or T-shirts with the words "Recovering Catholic" on them, hot items among some gay and lesbian activists? The implication that someone's religious faith is a mental illness is clearly an expression of contempt. If that isn't covered under the definition of hate speech, what is?

Or take the following sentence: "The act male homosexuals commit is ugly and repugnant and afterwards they are disgusted with themselves. They drink and take drugs to palliate this, but they are disgusted with the act and they are always changing partners and cannot be really happy." The thoughts of Pat Robertson or Patrick Buchanan? Actually that sentence was written by Gertrude Stein, one of the century's most notable lesbians. Or take the following, about how beating up "black boys like that made us feel *good* inside. . . . Every time I drove my foot into his [expletive], I felt better." It was written to describe the brutal assault of an innocent bystander for the sole reason of his race. By the end of the attack, the victim had blood gushing from his mouth as his attackers stomped on his genitals. Are we less appalled when we learn that the actual sentence was how beating up "white boys like that made us feel *good* inside. . . . Every time I drove my foot into his [expletive], I felt better?" It was written by Nathan McCall, an African-American who later in life became a successful journalist at the *Washington Post* and published his memoir of this "hate crime" to much acclaim.

In fact, one of the stranger aspects of hate is that the prejudice expressed by a group in power may often be milder in expression than the prejudice felt by the marginalized. After all, if you already enjoy privilege, you may not feel the anger that turns bias into hate. You may not need to. For this reason, most white racism may be more influential in society than most black racism—but also more calmly expressed.

So may other forms of minority loathing—especially hatred within minorities. I'm sure that black conservatives like Clarence Thomas or Thomas Sowell have experienced their fair share of white racism. But I wonder whether it has ever reached the level of intensity of the hatred directed toward them by other blacks? In several years of being an openly gay writer and editor, I have experienced the gamut of responses to my sexual orientation. But I have only directly experienced articulated, passionate hate from other homosexuals. I have been accused over the years by other homosexuals of being a sellout, a hypocrite, a traitor, a sexist, a racist, a narcissist, a snob. I've been called selfish, callous, hateful, self-hating and malevolent. At a reading, a group of lesbian activists portrayed my face on a poster within the crossfires of a gun. Nothing from the religious right has come close to such vehemence.

I am not complaining. No harm has ever come to me or my property, and much of the criticism is rooted in the legitimate expression of political differences. But the visceral tone and style of the gay criticism can only be described as hateful. It is designed to wound personally, and it often does. But its intensity comes in part, one senses, from the pain of being excluded for so long, of anger long restrained bubbling up and directing itself more aggressively toward an alleged traitor than an alleged enemy. It is the hate of the hated. And it can be the most hateful hate of all. For this reason, hate-crime laws may themselves be an oddly biased category—biased against the victims of hate. Racism is everywhere, but the already victimized might be more desperate, more willing to express it violently. And so more prone to come under the suspicious eye of the law.

The cardinal social sin

And why is hate for a group worse than hate for a person? In Laramie, Wyo., the now-famous epicenter of "homophobia," where Matthew Shepard was brutally beaten to death, vicious murders are not unknown. In the previous 12 months, a 15-year-old pregnant girl was found east of the town with 17 stab wounds. Her 38-year-old boyfriend was apparently angry that she had refused an abortion and left her in the Wyoming foothills to bleed to death. In the summer of 1998, an 8-year-old Laramie girl was abducted, raped and murdered by a pedophile, who disposed of her young body in a garbage dump. Neither of these killings was deemed a hate crime, and neither would be designated as such under any existing hate-crime law. Perhaps because of this, one crime is an international legend; the other two are virtually unheard of.

But which crime was more filled with hate? Once you ask the question, you realize how difficult it is to answer. Is it more hateful to kill a stranger or a lover? Is it more hateful to kill a child than an adult? Is it more hateful to kill your own child than another's? Under the law before the invention of hate crimes, these decisions didn't have to be taken. But under the law after hate crimes, a decision is essential. A decade ago, a murder was a murder. Now, in the era when group hate has emerged as our cardinal social sin, it all depends.

The supporters of laws against hate crimes argue that such crimes should be disproportionately punished because they victimize more than the victim. Such crimes, these advocates argue, spread fear, hatred and panic among whole populations, and therefore merit more concern. But, of course, all crimes victimize more than the victim, and spread alarm in the society at large. Just think of the terrifying church shooting in Texas in September 1999. In fact, a purely random murder may be even more terrifying than a targeted one, since the entire community, and not just a part of it, feels threatened. High rates of murder, robbery, assault and burglary victimize everyone, by spreading fear, suspicion and distress everywhere. Which crime was more frightening to more people in the summer of 1999: the mentally ill Buford Furrow's crazed attacks in Los Angeles, killing one, or Mark Barton's murder of his own family and several random day-traders in Atlanta, killing 12? Almost certainly the latter. But only Furrow was guilty of "hate."

One response to this objection is that certain groups feel fear more intensely than others because of a history of persecution or intimidation. But doesn't this smack of a certain condescension toward minorities? Why, after all, should it be assumed that gay men or black women or Jews, for example, are as a group more easily intimidated than others? Surely in any of these communities there will be a vast range of responses, from panic to concern to complete indifference. The assumption otherwise is the kind of crude generalization the law is supposed to uproot in the first place. And among these groups, there are also likely to be vast differences. To equate a population once subjected to slavery with a population of Mexican immigrants or third-generation Holocaust survivors is to equate the unequatable. In fact, it is to set up a contest of vulnerability in which one group vies with another to establish its particular variety of suffering, a contest that can have no dignified solution.

Rape, for example, is not classified as a "hate crime" under most existing laws, pitting feminists against ethnic groups in a battle for recognition. If, as a solution to this problem, everyone, except the white straight able-bodied male, is regarded as a possible victim of a hate crime, then we have simply created a two-tier system of justice in which racial profiling is reversed, and white straight men are presumed guilty before being proven innocent, and members of minorities are free to hate them as gleefully as they like. But if we include the white straight male in the litany of potential victims, then we have effectively abolished the notion of a hate crime altogether. For if every crime is possibly a hate crime, then it is simply another name for crime. All we will have done is widened the search for possible bigotry, ratcheted up the sentences for everyone and filled the jails up even further.

Hate-crime-law advocates counter that extra penalties should be imposed on hate crimes because our society is experiencing an "epidemic" of such crimes. Mercifully, there is no hard evidence to support this notion. The Federal Government has only been recording the incidence of hate crimes in this decade, and the statistics tell a simple story. In 1992, there were 6,623 hate-crime incidents reported to the F.B.I. by a total of 6,181 agencies, covering 51 percent of the population. In 1996, there were 8,734 incidents reported by 11,355 agencies, covering 84 percent of the population. That number dropped to 8,049 in 1997. These numbers are, of course, hazardous. They probably underreport the incidence of such crimes, but they are the only reliable figures we have. Yet even if they are faulty as an absolute number, they do not show an epidemic of "hate crimes" in the 1990's.

Is there evidence that the crimes themselves are becoming more vicious? None. More than 60 percent of recorded hate crimes in America involve no violent, physical assault against another human being at all, and, again, according to the F.B.I., that proportion has not budged much in the 1990's. These impersonal attacks are crimes against property or crimes of "intimidation." Murder, which dominates media coverage of hate crimes, is a tiny proportion of the total. Of the 8,049 hate crimes reported to the F.B.I. in 1997, a total of eight were murders. Eight. The number of hate crimes that were aggravated assaults (generally involving a weapon) in 1997 is less than 15 percent of the total. That's 1,237 assaults too many, of course, but to put it in perspective, compare it with a reported 1,022,492 "equal opportunity" aggravated assaults in America in the same year. The number of hate crimes that were physical assaults is half the total. That's 4,000 assaults too many, of course, but to put it in perspective, it compares with around 3.8 million "equal opportunity" assaults in America annually.

The truth is, the distinction between a crime filled with personal hate and a crime filled with group hate is an essentially arbitrary one. It tells us nothing interesting about the psychological contours of the specific actor or his specific victim. It is a function primarily of politics, of special interest groups carving out particular protections for themselves, rather than a serious response to a serious criminal concern. In such an endeavor, hate-crime-law advocates cram an entire world of human motivations into an immutable, tiny box called hate, and hope to have solved a problem. But nothing has been solved; and some harm may even have been done.

In an attempt to repudiate a past that treated people differently because of the color of their skin, or their sex, or religion or sexual orientation, we may merely create a future that permanently treats people differently because of the color of their skin, or their sex, religion or sexual orientation. This notion of a hate crime, and the concept of hate that lies behind it, takes a psychological mystery and turns it into a facile political artifact. Rather than compounding this error and extending it even further, we should seriously consider repealing the concept altogether.

Equanimity in the face of prejudice

To put it another way: Violence can and should be stopped by the government. In a free society, hate can't and shouldn't be. The boundaries between hate and prejudice and between prejudice and opinion and between opinion and truth are so complicated and blurred that any attempt to construct legal and political fire walls is a doomed and illiberal venture.

We know by now that hate will never disappear from human consciousness; in fact, it is probably, at some level, definitive of it. We know after decades of education measures that hate is not caused merely by ignorance; and after decades of legislation, that it isn't caused entirely by law.

To be sure, we have made much progress. Anyone who argues that America is as inhospitable to minorities and to women today as it has been in the past has not read much history. And we should, of course, be vigilant that our most powerful institutions, most notably the government, do not actively or formally propagate hatred; and insure that the violent expression of hate is curtailed by the same rules that punish all violent expression.

Hate is only foiled not when the haters are punished but when the hated are immune to the bigot's power.

But after that, in an increasingly diverse culture, it is crazy to expect that hate, in all its variety, can be eradicated. A free country will always mean a hateful country. This may not be fair, or perfect, or admirable, but it is reality, and while we need not endorse it, we should not delude ourselves into thinking we can prevent it. That is surely the distinction between toleration and tolerance. Tolerance is the eradication of hate; toleration is co-existence despite it. We might do better as a culture and as a polity if we concentrated more on achieving the latter rather than the former. We would certainly be less frustrated.

And by aiming lower, we might actually reach higher. In some ways, some expression of prejudice serves a useful social purpose. It lets off steam; it allows natural tensions to express themselves incrementally; it can siphon off conflict through words, rather than actions. Anyone who has lived in the ethnic shouting match that is New York City knows exactly what I mean. If New Yorkers disliked each other less, they wouldn't be able to get on so well. We may not all be able to pull off a Mencken—bigoted in words, egalitarian in action—but we might achieve a lesser form of virtue: a human acceptance of our need for differentiation, without a total capitulation to it.

Do we not owe something more to the victims of hate? Perhaps we do. But it is also true that there is nothing that government can do for the hated that the hated cannot better do for themselves. After all, most bigots are not foiled when they are punished specifically for their beliefs. In fact, many of the worst haters crave such attention and find vindication in such rebukes. Indeed, our media's obsession with "hate," our elevation of it above other social misdemeanors and crimes, may even play into the hands of the pathetic and the evil, may breathe air into the smoldering embers of their paranoid loathing. Sure, we can help create a climate in which such hate is disapproved of—and we should. But there is a danger that if we go too far, if we punish it too much, if we try to abolish it altogether, we may merely increase its mystique, and entrench the very categories of human difference that we are trying to erase.

For hate is only foiled not when the haters are punished but when the hated are immune to the bigot's power. A hater cannot psychologically wound if a victim cannot psychologically be wounded. And that immunity to hurt can never be given; it can merely be achieved. The racial epithet only strikes at someone's core if he lets it, if he allows the bigot's definition of him to be the final description of his life and his person—if somewhere in his heart of hearts, he believes the hateful slur to be true. The only final answer to this form of racism, then, is not majority persecution of it, but minority indifference to it. The only permanent rebuke to homophobia is not the enforcement of tolerance, but gay equanimity in the face of prejudice. The only effective answer to sexism is not a morass of legal proscriptions, but the simple fact of female success. In this, as in so many other things, there is no solution to the problem. There is only a transcendence of it. For all our rhetoric, hate will never be destroyed. Hate, as our predecessors knew better, can merely be overcome.

4

Many Hate Crimes Are Hoaxes

John Leo

John Leo is a columnist for the U.S. News and World Report.

The recent frenzy of press and political rhetoric surrounding hate crimes has led some college students to fake hate-based incidents. For example, two weeks after the fatal beating of gay student Matthew Shepard in 1998, a lesbian student in St. Cloud, Minnesota, claimed that two men harassed her with antigay remarks and slashed her face. Before she confessed to faking the crime, students raised $12,000 as a reward for information about her assailants. People commit such hoaxes to prove that college life is a hostile environment for minority students and women and to forward the agendas of campus interest groups.

For three weeks in the spring of 2000, minority students at the University of Iowa's College of Dentistry were the targets of menacing E-mail and a bomb threat. Red noodles were left on the doorstep of a black student, with a note suggesting that they represented a dead black person's brain. Surveillance tapes were set up. The FBI located the computer used in the E-mail threats. A black dental student, Tarsha Michelle Claiborne, was arrested and confessed.

In the midst of an antirape rally at the University of Massachusetts, a woman cut herself with a knife, tossed it under a car, and then walked across the street, claiming to be a victim of sexual assault. After nearly a month of negotiations between police and her attorney, she admitted that she had made up the whole thing. This was the fourth in a series of reported sexual assaults at the school. In one of the previous three, a woman said she fought off three male attackers and ran for help after being hit with "a pepper-spray-like substance." This may well be true, but some people on campus believe it's hard to fight off three assailants and harder still to escape at all after a chemical spraying.

Campuses are developing new doubts about reports of race and gender crimes. In 1999, the *Chronicle of Higher Education* published a roundup of campus hoaxes, cautioning that this "flurry of fabrications doesn't necessarily suggest a trend." But it certainly looks like a trend. Race and gender are the dominant concerns at colleges today. Sometimes the temptation to prove that racism and sexism pervade campus life leads people to fake incidents. At Spokane Community College, a racist and sexist letter from "Whitey" appeared in an advice column in the student newspaper, the *Reporter*, in 1999. After campus protests about the letter's derogatory language about women, gays, and minority students, the newspaper's editors admitted that "Whitey" was a fictional character they had created to raise awareness about racism on campus. Jerry Kennedy, a gay resident assistant at the University of Georgia, reported he had been the target of nine hate crimes over a period of three years, including three acts of arson. But during questioning, Kennedy admitted that he had set the fires.

Campuses are developing new doubts about reports of race and gender crimes.

Caught in the act. Two weeks after the murder of Matthew Shepard [in 1998], a lesbian student at St. Cloud State University in Minnesota said two men shouted antigay slurs at her and then slashed her face. Outraged students raised nearly $12,000 as a reward for information about her attackers. Then the student confessed she had made up the story and cut her own face. In a similar incident, a lesbian student at Eastern New Mexico University said she had been attacked after her name was included with the names of seven professors on an antigay "hit list" posted at a local laundromat. Police arrested her after a surveillance camera at the laundromat showed her posting the list.

Without a confession, convictions are rare. Two black students at Miami University in Ohio were accused of posting 55 racist and antigay fliers and typing racist computer messages. Their fingerprints and palm prints were found on 42 of the 55 fliers, but the defense argued that they had touched the papers when they were blank and someone else must have printed and posted the fliers. The jury acquitted.

Dubious reports pay off

Sometimes even dubious reports of race and gender offenses pay off, leading to an institutional payoff (more minority jobs or titles, more money for women's studies). Molly Martin, president of the student senate at North Carolina's Guilford College, said she had been assaulted, with the words "nigger lover" scrawled on her chest. Martin, who is white, had endorsed a proposal to create a full-time director of African-American affairs on campus. Police dropped the case, calling Martin "a reluctant witness." She later dropped out of Guilford and apologized for "acts that were inappropriate and that were injurious" to the college. She insisted that the attack had taken place but declined to say what acts she was apologizing for. Though many people on campus think the attack never took place, Martin achieved her goal: Guilford installed a director of African-American affairs.

One symptom of the truth problem

Like Tawana Brawley's hoax, some recent fake hate crimes seem intended to cover personal embarrassment. [In 1987, Brawley, a fifteen-year-old African American girl, falsely reported being raped by six white policemen to explain why she had missed her curfew.] Such was the case with a black student at Hastings College in Nebraska, who said he had been forced into a car by whites and dropped far out of town. He was cited for filing a false police report. But more of the college hoaxes seem to reflect an acted-out commitment to a cause, not just personal difficulties. One factor is that colleges now stress the need for each identity group to express its "voice" or "narrative," without much scruple about whether the narratives are literally true. (Postmodern theory says there is no such thing as truth anyway.) After the Brawley hoax, an article in the *Nation* magazine argued that it "doesn't matter" whether Brawley was lying, since the pattern of whites abusing blacks is true. And when Rigoberta Menchu's famous account of class and ethnic warfare in Guatemala was revealed to be largely false, many professors said this didn't matter much because her book contained emotional truth. The blurring of the line between fact and fiction is far advanced in our university culture. Hoaxes are just one symptom of the truth problem.

5

The Definition of Hate Crimes Should Be Expanded

Eric Holder

Eric Holder was Assistant U.S. Attorney General during the Clinton administration.

The Federal Hate Crimes Statute states that crimes motivated by race, color, religion, or national origin are subject to federal jurisdiction. However, this statute is insufficient because it only pertains to hate crime victims participating in a federally protected activity during the attack and does not apply to crimes based on sexual orientation, gender, or disability. Unfortunately, the true scope of these crimes as a growing national problem is just being realized. Hence, it is important that all hate crime victims are equally protected. Legislation should be enacted to expand the definition of hate crimes to include gays, women, and the disabled and fight the epidemic of hate crimes.

The battle against hate crimes has always been bipartisan, and this committee, [the House Judiciary Committee on Hate Crimes,] has always been at the forefront of that battle.

In 1990 and 1994, the committee strongly supported the enactment of the Hate Crimes Statistics Act and the Hate Crimes Sentencing Enhancement Act. In 1996, the committee responded in time of great national need by quickly [passing] the Church Arson Prevention Act.

And I hope that you will respond once again to the call for a stronger federal stand against hate crimes, and that you will join law enforcement officials and community leaders across the country in support of H.R. 1082, the Hate Crimes Prevention Act of 1999. [The bill did not pass.]

Now unfortunately, recent events have only reinforced the need for federal hate crimes legislation. We were all horrified at the brutal murders of Billy Jack Gaither in Alabama, Matthew Shepard in Wyoming and James Byrd in Jasper, Texas.

Just in the weeks since I testified on these issues before the Senate Judiciary Committee in May 1999, a young man linked with a white su-

Excerpted from the congressional testimony given by Assistant U.S. Attorney General, Eric Holder, before the House Judiciary Committee on Hate Crimes, August 4, 1999, Washington, D.C.

premacy organization shot several people in Illinois and Indiana, including a group of Jewish men walking home from sabbath services in Chicago. Two others died from their injuries: Won-Joon Yoon, a student at Indiana University from South Korea, and Ricky Byrdsong, an African-American male who was only walking with his daughters near his home in Skokie, Illinois.

In California, three synagogues in Sacramento erupted in flames on the same morning, and Winfield Scott Mowder and Gary Matson, a gay couple, were brutally murdered in their Redding home.

A problem for our country

These crimes, and others around the country, are not just a law enforcement problem. They are a problem for our schools, our religious institutions, our civic organizations and also for our national leaders.

When we pool our expertise, experiences and resources together, we can help build communities that are safer, stronger and more tolerant.

First, we must gain a better understanding of the problem. In 1997, the last year for which we have complete statistics, 11,200 law enforcement agencies participated in the data-collection program and reported just over 8,000 hate crime incidents. Eight-thousand hate crime incidents are about one hate crime incident per hour.

But we know that even this disturbing number significantly underestimates the true level of hate crimes. Many victims do not report these crimes, and police departments do not always recognize, appropriately categorize or adequately report hate crimes.

Violent hate crimes committed because of bias based on the victim's sexual orientation, gender or disability . . . pose a serious problem for our nation.

Second, we must learn to teach tolerance in our communities so that we can prevent hate crimes by addressing bias before it manifests itself in violent criminal activity. We must foster understanding and should instill in our children the respect for each other's differences and the ability to resolve conflicts without violence.

The Department of Education, with the National Association of Attorneys General, recently published a guide to confronting and stopping hate and bias in our schools. And I'm also pleased that the department is assisting a new partnership in its efforts to develop a program for middle school students on tolerance and diversity.

Third, we must work together to effectively prevent and prosecute hate crimes.

Now the centerpiece of the [Clinton] administration's hate crimes initiative is the formation of local working groups in the United States attorneys' districts around the country. These task forces are hard at work bringing together the FBI, the U.S. Attorney's Office, the Community Relations Service, local law enforcement, community leaders and educators to assess the problem in their area and to coordinate our response to hate crimes.

These cooperative efforts are reinforced by the July 1998 memorandum of understanding between the National District Attorneys Association and the Department of Justice. Where the federal government does have jurisdiction, the MOU [Memorandum of Understanding] calls for early communication among local, state and federal prosecutors to devise investigative strategies.

Finally, we should never forget that law enforcement has an indispensable role to play in eradicating hate crimes. We must ensure that potential hate crimes are investigated thoroughly, prosecuted swiftly and punished soundly. In order to do this effectively, we must address the gaps that exist in the current federal law.

Current statute has serious deficiencies

The principal Federal Hate Crimes Statute, 18 USC Section 245, prohibits certain hate crimes committed on the basis of race, color, religion or national origin. This law has two serious deficiencies.

First, even in the most blatant cases of racial, ethnic or religious violence, no federal jurisdiction exists unless the violence was committed because the victim engaged in one of six federally protected activities. This unnecessary, extra intent requirement has led to acquittals in several cases. It has also limited our ability to work with state and local officials to investigate and prosecute many incidents of brutal, hate-motivated violence.

Any federal legislative response to hate crimes must close this gap.

H.R. 1082 would amend Section 245 so that in cases involving racial, religious or ethnic violence, the federal government would have the jurisdiction to investigate and prosecute cases involving the intentional infliction of bodily injury without regard for the victim's participation in one of the six enumerated federally protected activities.

And as I said, this is an essential fix. In my written testimony, I highlight several cases that we have lost because of the federally protected activity burden.

We can offer [assistance] to these localities, but in most circumstances, only if we have jurisdiction in the first instance. The level of collaboration achieved between federal and local officials in Jasper, with regard to the James Byrd case, was possible only because we had a colorable claim of federal jurisdiction in that matter. The state and federal partnership in this case led to the prompt inditement of three men on state capital charges.

The second jurisdictional limitation on Section 245 is that it provides no coverage whatsoever for violent hate crimes committed because of bias based on the victim's sexual orientation, gender or disability, and these crimes pose a serious problem for our nation.

Federal response is needed

A meaningful federal response to hate crimes must provide protection for these groups, and H.R. 282 would do just that. The bill would prohibit the intentional infliction of bodily injury based on the victim's sexual orientation, gender or disability whenever the incident involved or affected interstate commerce.

And we know that a significant number of hate crimes based on the sexual orientation of the victim are committed every year in this country. And despite this fact, 18 U.S.C. 245 does not provide coverage for these victims unless there is independent basis for federal jurisdiction.

We also know that a significant number of women are exposed to brutality and even death because of their gender. The Congress, with the enactment of the Violence Against Women Act in 1994, has recognized that some violent assaults committed against women are bias crimes rather than mere random attacks.

And we also know that because of their concern about the problem of disability-related hate crimes, Congress amended the Hate Crimes Statistics Act in 1994 to require the FBI to collect information about such hate-based incidents from state and local law enforcement agencies.

It is by working in collaboration that state and federal law enforcement officials stand the best chance of bringing the perpetrators of hate crimes swiftly to justice.

Similarly, the federal sentencing guidelines include an upward adjustment for crimes where the victim was selected because of his or her sexual orientation, gender or disability.

H.R. 1082 is consistent with recent court decisions on Congress' legislative power under Section 5 of the 14th Amendment and is mindful of commerce clause limitations.

Congress has the constitutional authority to regulate violent acts motivated by racial or ethnic bias. The bill is also mindful of the traditional role that states have played in prosecuting crime.

Indeed, state and local officials investigate and prosecute the vast majority of the hate crimes that occur in their communities and would continue to do so if this bill was enacted.

But we need to make sure that federal jurisdiction covers everything that it should, so that in those rare instances where states cannot or will not take action, the federal government can step in to assure that justice is done.

It is by working in collaboration that state and federal law enforcement officials stand the best chance of bringing the perpetrators of hate crimes swiftly to justice.

The Hate Crimes Prevention Act will bring together state, local and federal teams to investigate and prosecute incidents of hate crime wherever they occur.

The enactment of H.R. 1082 is a reasonable measure and a necessary response to the wave of hate-based incidents taking place around our country because of biases built on the race, color, national origin, religion, sexual orientation, gender or disability of the victim.

6

The Definition of Hate Crimes Should Not Be Expanded

Fred Dickey

Fred Dickey is a contributing writer to the Los Angeles Times Magazine.

Expanding the definition of hate crimes would create more problems than solutions. For instance, the vast majority of hate crimes are not committed by vigilant members of extremist groups, but by habitual troublemakers. Enhancing hate crime laws would inadvertently send more young, undereducated, poor, mentally ill men to prison. In addition, the small number of hate crime prosecutions does not necessitate the expansion of hate crime laws. Existing criminal justice policies sufficiently deal with hate crimes. Furthermore, extending extra federal protection to certain groups creates a special class of victims and undermines the equality of all Americans.

Billy McCall is a man of dubious distinction. He is the first man in the nation convicted of a hate crime against women, says his San Diego County prosecutor. Regrettably, this 29-year-old black man is not the first person convicted of a "hate crime" unjustly.

In September 1999, in a scene captured on a Macy's department store security camera, McCall approached a young woman and tried to make conversation. She walked briskly away. He followed her, talking rapidly, then shoved her into a table of shoes. She stumbled, regained her footing and turned to face him. McCall took a few steps toward her, then swerved away and departed.

The young woman was Yvonne Bejarano, 18-year-old daughter of David Bejarano, San Diego's police chief. After San Diego television stations repeatedly aired the video, four other women came forward to charge that McCall had publicly abused them, too, with assaults ranging from yanking their hair to knocking one of them to the pavement. McCall was found guilty of five counts of assault and battery and sentenced to four years. Jurors also convicted him of a hate crime, adding two years to his term.

The love affair with hate crimes

At his trial, Hector Jimenez, the deputy district attorney in charge of hate crime prosecution for San Diego County, told the court: "Unless this defendant receives a serious penalty under the law for his crime, the court will have transmitted the message that this crime is not important in society's list of priorities. He's not some unguided missile who will hit anyone and everything. He only hits attractive women when he's angry. . . ."

The phrase "attractive women" was pivotal, because under the hate crime laws proliferating around the country, "hate" must be directed at a particular group: racial, ethnic, religious, gender. But Billy McCall, as it happens, is an equal opportunity hater. He's an angry man capable of lashing out at anyone at any time. "Billy needs help," says his mother, Shelley Julian. "He has this tremendous anger that just comes over him. He can't seem to help himself. If you, or anybody, were standing across the street and Billy thought you were staring at him, he'd be over there in a flash, and you'd better have a good explanation. He gets in fights all the time."

Indeed, McCall had been imprisoned before—for violence against men as well as women—and just before being charged with hating women only, he was arrested for attacking his 19-year-old brother, inflicting a facial cut that required 13 stitches. Prosecutors did not charge him for that crime because it would have contradicted their argument that McCall hated women specifically, says his attorney, Karolyn E. Kovtun of San Diego.

McCall clearly is a menace, one who deserves punishment—and who undoubtedly needs psychological help. Does it matter that he is serving extra time for hating women? What's important is that McCall is off the streets. Yet his case is troubling if you believe in justice in the largest sense, if you realize McCall's experience is repeated across the country, and if you consider what the nation's recent love affair with hate crime laws truly has wrought.

An easy sell

Hate crime legislation has been an easy sell to legislatures and the public because of a general belief that the laws will primarily punish synagogue bombers and Klan murderers, who are almost always dealt with severely anyway. Instead, the offenders commonly nailed by these laws are poor and uneducated whites and minorities whose offenses often are closer to throwing punches than bombs. Intended to send a signal that violence against racial, ethnic or religious groups is no longer tolerable in America, the laws instead are being used by prosecutors in questionable circumstances to demonstrate that they are tough on hate. Intended to give some measure of protection to historical victims of racism, the laws instead are being expanded to cover an ever-lengthening list of victims groups.

Former Los Angeles County D.A. Ira Reiner advocated hate crime laws while he was in office, from 1984 to 1992. He lobbied for them to end hate activities and conspiracies as practiced primarily by groups attempting to impose their agenda on society through terror and violence, especially by targeting minorities. Instead, he says, hate crime laws have become the captive of victims groups and prosecutors who buckle under their pressure. "The hijacking of hate crime legislation occurred when every victims group decided to validate their status by having their group added to the list. I guess if you're not on the list, you're a second-class victims group."

John Jackson, supervisor of academic instruction for the California Department of Corrections, says simply that in California, "The Legislature has gone completely mad."

Identity politics

In 1987, California was one of the first states to enact a hate crime statute. It passed handily with bipartisan support. The original law added extra punishment for crimes motivated by race, color, religion, ancestry, national origin and sexual orientation of the victims. Through the years, the list broadened to include gender, disability and mistaken attacks—which means if a heterosexual is assumed to be gay and is attacked, it is a hate crime, or if a white person is confused for a Hispanic and targeted, it is a hate crime. California law also includes a "special circumstance" provision to allow some murders committed as hate crimes to be punishable by death.

As the laws raced through legislatures around the country, there were few voices of dissent. In the lexicon of magic political words, being against hate is abracadabra. Can you imagine a candidate trying to defend against a 30-second commercial accusing him or her of being "soft on hate?"

Intended to give some measure of protection to historical victims of racism, the [hate crime] laws instead are being expanded to cover an ever-lengthening list of victims groups.

Today, 45 states, the District of Columbia and the federal government have some form of hate crime laws, and Congress is debating expansion of the federal laws. As the legislation was debated, many liberals were excited, and conservatives were mute. Doubts from 1st Amendment advocates and those who feared increased social divisions were drowned out by pressure groups. Advocates cited, at one time or another, four reasons for the laws: deterrence, protection for members of victims groups, compassion for traditional targets of hate and the making of a political statement that hate crimes will not be tolerated. They promised a high barrier to protect against prosecutors who would try defendants for their political or social beliefs, rather than for their actions.

The supporters tend to be gay-rights organizations, some minority groups, the Anti-Defamation League and other organizations dedicated to identity politics, says Gail Heriot, a professor at the University of San Diego School of Law. "These people want to be able to write home to their memberships and say, 'Look what I did for you.'"

The ACLU generally has favored the laws, although many of its members have waffled, torn between their loyalties to traditional liberal allies and their misgivings about the specter of "thought crimes" suddenly being brought before the bar of justice. The laws also enjoyed largely unquestioning support from the media.

The hardcore menace?

According to the State of California, Michael Ostrow is an anti-Semite. Caught and convicted.

At 4 p.m. on April 28, 1997, a frail 76-year-old man and his wife hastily departed a bus at Sunset Boulevard and Highland Avenue in Los Angeles and started across the street. They were followed by Ostrow, 57, a stranger to them. Ostrow repeatedly cursed the old man as a "dirty Jew." Moments before, he had shouted a similar insult at a woman passenger on the bus. Suddenly, Ostrow pushed the man, knocking him to the ground and breaking his hip.

Months later in court, as this "anti-Semite" was about to be sentenced for assault and a hate crime, his public defender, Ilona Peltyn, revealed an astonishing fact: "Mr. Ostrow was born Jewish. His mother is Jewish and lives in Israel. His sister is Jewish. Mr. Ostrow is now Catholic," his attorney concluded, "but he loves his mother."

Prosecutor Carla Arranaga, deputy district attorney in charge of the Hate Crimes Suppression Unit, was anything but alarmed by the disclosure. "Most of the hate crime cases I handle are committed by individuals who attack their very own," she told the court. "This is not unusual, the fact that he is of the same ethnicity."

Statistics do not bear out Arranaga's claim. But if correct, it would mean Los Angeles County is using hate crime laws to prosecute those who prey on their own race, gender, ethnicity and so on. It's hard to imagine this is what the advocates of hate crime laws had in mind. DNA civil rights attorney Peter Neufeld whimsically observes, "Apparently, they're not hate crimes anymore, they're self-hate crimes."

As do most impoverished defendants, Ostrow plea-bargained and was sentenced to six years, which broke down to four years for battery with serious bodily injury and two years for the hate crime enhancement. Afterward, someone close to Ostrow offered an unadorned explanation for his behavior. Ostrow, the person said, "is nuts," and his instability extends to his religious conversion.

Like McCall, Ostrow deserved punishment. But also like McCall, Ostrow hardly seems the hard-core menace that advocates of the laws had in mind. He does, however, count as a conviction, and that is no small thing in a climate where D.A.s are wise to show toughness.

The Los Angeles County Human Relations Commission's 1999 "Hate Crimes Report" claimed that hate crimes in the county had risen 11.7% from the previous year. The announcement led to a bevy of headlines and newscasts, giving the impression that the county was experiencing a hate crime epidemic. The commission warned that the rising number of crimes "erodes the public's perception that schools, places of business and homes are safe environments, protected from hate crime."

A close look at the statistics, however, shows that in this county of 10 million people, the most polyglot population on the face of the earth, the number of alleged—that's alleged, mind you—hate crimes for 1999 was 859. These were incidents reported by police, activist groups and schools. Of that total, 98 resulted in felony charges, and 102 were cases against juveniles. To be sure, one true hate crime is too many. But as crime waves go, this one seemed more like a ripple.

The commission's report also said that the most violent hate crimes "tended to be race-based and were largely caused by racially motivated gang activity." In other words, statistics from the most crime-prone element of society, a segment never known for much tolerance toward anyone, were used to define Los Angeles as a community of rising hate.

American justice, when applied fairly, has no problems punishing criminals motivated by hate even without the new [hate crime] laws.

The report also showed there were 10 times more hate crimes on the Westside (342 per 1 million people) than in the west San Gabriel Valley (33 per 1 million). Is hatred really 10 times worse on the Westside? It seems more likely that the politically liberal Westside is more attuned to what Kovtun calls "the designer crime of the moment, the latest political correctness crime," and that authorities there are eager to appear responsive.

As for those committing the crimes, Christopher Plourd, a San Diego criminal defense lawyer who has represented six clients charged with hate crimes, says, "It is demonstrable that these laws hit the poor and minorities hardest. It wasn't meant that way, but that's the way it is." The L.A. County District Attorney's Office says that in 1999 it filed charges against 38 whites and 41 members of minority groups—31 Latinos, 8 blacks and 2 Asians.

Nationwide, FBI statistics show that there were 6,305 hate crimes reported against persons in 1998. Of those, more than half were classified as "intimidation," which meant they stopped short of violence.

At the federal level, the Justice Department says that it has filed an average of five federal hate crime charges a year for each of the last five years. Despite that small number of prosecutions, legislation pending in Congress would expand the law to include acts motivated by gender, sexual orientation and disability. [The legislation did not pass.] The latter group is included even though the most recent statistics show that just 25 alleged hate crimes against the disabled were reported by the 50 states in 1999—two in California and none in L.A. County. The question those minuscule figures raise is whether there is need for special protection, especially since an attack on a blind man or a woman in a wheelchair has always tended to put sentencing judges in a nasty mood.

In fact, American justice, when applied fairly, has no problem punishing criminals motivated by hate even without the new laws. In California, sentencing guidelines fall into three categories: low, medium and high. For example, assault and battery by two or more people carries a low sentence of two years and a high sentence of four. On top of such underlying sentences, a hate crime conviction can add a maximum of four years. But in practice, the sentence often does not exceed the maximum for the primary offense. Instead, plea bargains routinely reflect a low or medium sentence for the primary crime, then an enhancement for the hate crime.

Noble—and naive—purposes

Advocates of hate crime laws have noble purposes that go beyond simply locking up thugs. The purpose is also to deter haters from striking out and to offer some comfort to victims by demonstrating that authorities are especially tough on hate crimes.

If only it were so easy. "It's silly and naive to think the threat of longer sentences will stop people who commit these crimes," says Peltyn, a Los Angeles public defender for over 20 years. "It's not like they spend their time studying new legislation. They don't even know there are such laws. Do we really think that knowing there was a hate crime penalty would have stopped Buford Furrow?" she says, referring to the man accused of shooting five people at a Los Angeles Jewish community center and killing an Asian postal worker in 1999.

Peltyn says hate crime laws are ineffective because many defendants are people with disordered thinking. "Lots of them are mentally ill. They get tried as though they're normal because they manage to appear that way. They know they're in court and they understand the charges; they can even sound like they're making sense much of the time, but it's part of their illness that they refuse to admit they're sick, so they go to prison."

As for the solace that hate crime laws could give victims, Beverly Hills forensic psychiatrist Ronald Markman says, "We can't predict how a crime victim will deal with his or her trauma. Legislation alone won't give a person comfort." Recent research into that question reached a surprising conclusion. Victims of hate violence aren't any more traumatized than victims of non-hate crimes, and actually adjust better in sustaining self-esteem, wrote Arnold Barnes of Indiana University and Paul H. Ephross of the University of Maryland at Baltimore in a report published by the journal *Social Work*.

"If you say it's worse to kill someone because he's black, then you're saying it's not as bad to kill someone because he's not."

Susan Fisher, executive director of the Doris Tate Crime Victims Bureau, a statewide victims-rights group, says, "To assume that the emotional shock of crime hits certain groups harder than others is simply not true, and was undoubtedly said by someone who has never been a victim of a violent crime. You would never hear the mother of a murdered child say that the death of her child was less important than someone else's. Violent crime is violent crime, no matter whom it is directed against."

Consider the ironies. A Latino who murders a white man because of his race could be given the death penalty under hate crime laws. Yet if the same killer murdered a Latino child for "sport," he would not get the death penalty.

Those kinds of distinctions have a "tendency to Balkanize criminal law," says Jonathan Rauch, who often writes about gay issues. "The message we ought to be sending is that violence is intolerable, period. If you say it's worse to kill someone because he's black, then you're saying it's not as bad to kill someone because he's not."

The effect has been to enhance racial and other divisions, not ease them. "Hate crime laws are symptomatic of society's Balkanization," says Jonathan Kozol, author and children's advocate. "They are futile in the long run. We cannot rebuild society by legislative penalties for insensitive acts and utterances."

That's true even for those convicted of hate crimes because, unfortunately, prisons are ripe settings to polish hating skills. For example, says Jackson, the Department of Corrections official: "Let's say Convict A comes in here convicted of armed robbery. If he keeps his nose clean and minds his own business, he can serve out his time without much trouble. However, if Convict B is convicted of armed robbery plus a hate crime against one of the main groups in here, if word of that gets out on the main line—and there's a good chance it will—he's going to have to join a hate group of his own race just to survive. When he leaves here, he's going to be a lot better hater than when he came in."

Does the prison system try to help those convicted of hate crimes? Jackson replies matter of factly: "We don't have a program in here to address that."

No definition of hate

On almost every night of his life, Morgan Manduley has been a normal boy of 15. But on July 5, 2000, he may also have been a mean and stupid kid. Manduley and seven other boys, ages 14 to 17, all from comfortable San Diego homes, are accused of robbing and beating a group of elderly Latino farm workers during a "wilding" in which police say they vowed to attack some "beaners." If the charges are true, Manduley and his buds wanted some kicks with no risks, so they picked on old men who couldn't fight back and couldn't call for help. That suggests a motive closer to cowardice than racial animus, yet all eight were arrested and face charges for their cruel and senseless act that include hate crimes because the victims were Latino. Manduley faces a maximum sentence of 13 years.

To lock away Manduley's white companions with the "hates Latinos" label might well force them to seek haven with a white hate group. Where Manduley would turn for protection, however, is a riddle because he is Latino. Think about that for a moment. Not only does the hate crime charge mean prosecutors are pressing another "self-loathing" prosecution, but they are also asking us to accept a mental high-wire act that raises such questions as: If the seven white kids hate Latinos, why were they hanging out with Manduley? If you hate some Latinos but not others, can you be accused of hating an entire race? Perhaps they hate Latinos but run with Manduley because he's into self-loathing?

The distinctions and contradictions numb the mind. Ponder them long enough and inevitably you will arrive at a single central question:

What is hate?

There is no agreed-upon definition; there is no psychiatric definition at all. Historically, our criminal justice system has avoided asking prosecutors and jurors to define hate as a motive. The issue is whether or not the defendant broke the law, not why.

"Traditionally, motive was used as an investigative tool or to aid the judge in passing sentence," says Steve Carroll, head public defender of San Diego County. "Now it becomes part of the crime. This is turning the system upside down."

Jurors are asked to weigh types and degrees of hate, in effect, to read minds. Perhaps that is the biggest flaw in these well-meaning statutes. They ask for judgments in such vague realms that they are open to abuse by authorities, and to gaping inconsistencies. For example, we have long been told that rape is not an act of sex, but of power and of hatred toward women. Why then is rape almost never prosecuted as a hate crime? Here is prosecutor Arranaga's answer:

"We have not prosecuted a rape as a hate crime because we would have to prove that the victim's gender was a substantial motivation. We have cases of rape where men have raped men, men have raped women, and women have engaged in sexual misconduct, which is motivated by the gender of the victim, but is a more exploitative crime of violence and dominating control. And we can't prove that all rapes are gender based."

Thought crimes and hate crimes

The great lament of libertarians is that the thin line between "thought crimes" and hate crimes has been obscured as law enforcement scrambles after the haters. "What a hate crime charge allows the district attorney to do is say, in effect, 'We can't get you for more than a misdemeanor, but we don't like what you believe in so we're going to punish you by charging you with a hate crime and elevate it to a felony,'" says Kovtun, McCall's attorney. "The statute is extraordinarily vague. Even the jury instructions are vague. The conduct is not defined. The D.A. has all the power. Once he charges something, the court is going to ratify it in the preliminary hearing; that's almost automatic."

Although many prosecutors insist they aren't "thought police," many cases indicate otherwise.

In Lancaster in 1997, a group of white youths fired a shotgun at a car carrying African Americans. The act itself was not disputed, but Arranaga told the court: The defendants "regularly referred to African Americans in derogatory terms. When he saw an African American, Jason Deal would say, 'Look, there is a stupid, f——— nigger. . . .' Michael Bryant admitted to being a white supremacist. He and Thomas Deal kept Confederate flags in their bedrooms. Jason Deal likewise admitted he believed in the separation of the races."

In a justice system now accustomed to hate crimes, such evidence no longer raises many eyebrows. But it does elsewhere. "It is outrageous when evidence like that can be used in court just to stir people's emotions," says Heriot of University of San Diego School of Law.

Despite claims to the contrary, prosecutors must pursue such evidence if they are to prove hate crimes. "It's inevitable that when prosecutors have a weak case on a hate crime charge, they'll send investigators out to ask, 'What did this guy say 10 years ago about . . .?'" says civil libertarian and columnist Nat Hentoff. So prosecutors look at what defendants read, whom they associate with, what flags they have on their walls. If you are charged with a hate crime for beating up a Christian boy, it's best to hide your Koran.

Curiously, hate crime laws also turn on end a fundamental tenet of American courts: Jurors are almost always forbidden from knowing about a defendant's prior convictions. "In such cases, the fear is that juries will judge defendants because of who they are, and will convict on the basis of what has been done in the past, and that strikes directly at the right to a fair trial," says Loyola law professor Stan Goldman. Yet, under hate crime laws, prosecutors can portray someone's past as that of a loathsome bigot—precisely for the purpose of predisposing the jury to convict.

"You get tougher treatment if you're charged with a hate crime," defense attorney Plourd says. "The basic crime is no different, but you become a target. They use that hate crime mentality in trial to scare the jury into convicting you. Prosecutors make examples out of people, and if you get picked to be an example, you're in big trouble." In San Diego, Plourd attributes much of this attitude to prosecutor Jimenez. "Hector's a zealot. It's scary. As a person, he's decent, but he's just overbearing when it comes to hate crime. He sees it everywhere."

Finally, there is this question: Where is the line between actions rooted in "hatred" and those stemming from the tensions and strife that arise from people rubbing against people who seem strange acting and strange looking? It seems unlikely that an unworldly farmer living in Jalisco, Mexico, would harbor dislike for blacks. Yet let that farmer move to Compton, next door to African Americans who may have their own resentments against funny-talking immigrants "taking over their town," and it would come as no shock that our new neighbors might start forming some mutual fear and anger. Perhaps a misunderstanding between neighbors erupts into violence. Is it truly a hate crime?

Every person equal?

Although bigotry and hate are far from extinguished, the United States has become more inclusive in recent generations. Americans deserve credit for lowering racial, ethnic and religious barriers to equality. Yet people do still engage in crimes based on hate. They are most often committed by undereducated or poverty-stricken or mentally screwed-up losers whose fate it is to fall into society's criminal justice cement mixer. There they can be punished by laws that were adequate long before hate crime statutes sprang up, and by judges who have always had the power to consider motive when fixing punishment. The idea that a separate set of hate crime laws would somehow dissuade them from doing what they do is as weak as the now-quaint idea that capital punishment lowers the murder rate.

A large stone in the foundation of the American dream is the idea that every person is equal in citizenship and that every life should be equally valued and equally protected. No one should accept less, but is anyone entitled to more?

7

Hate Speech Is a Hate Crime

Richard Delgado and Jean Stefancic

Richard Delgado is the Charles Inglis Thomson Professor of Law at the University of Colorado. Jean Stefancic is a research associate and a documents librarian at the University of Colorado School of Law. Delgado and Stefancic are the authors of Must We Defend Nazis?

Hate speech is speech that degrades or offends a person or group. It harms entire groups and communities, not just individuals. Many defenders of the First Amendment claim that enduring hate speech, from slurs to racist rhetoric, is the unsettling compromise that must be made in order to protect all forms of speech. However, masking hate speech as a constitutional right only permits the systematic denigration of marginalized people. It allows those in power to continually subjugate women, minorities, and other subordinate groups. Hate speech can no longer be tolerated. The United States should follow the lead of other nations that have proved that such speech can be outlawed without restricting free speech.

The argument that we must protect the speech we hate in order to protect that which we hold dear is a special favorite of certain commentators who advocate an unfettered First Amendment. For example, Samuel Walker, the author of a recent history of the ACLU[1] and another of the hate-speech controversy, writes that the ACLU believes that "every view, no matter how ignorant or harmful we may regard it, has a legal and moral right to be heard."[2] He explains that banning ignorant and hateful propaganda against Jews, for instance, "could easily lead to the suppression of other ideas now regarded as moderate and legitimate."[3] The free speech victories that have been won in defending Nazi and other unpopular speech, Walker points out, have also been used to protect pro–civil rights messages.[4] In two recent books and a series of law review articles, Nadine Strossen, the president of the ACLU, echoes Walker's views. "If the freedom of speech is weakened for one person, group, or message," according to Strossen, we will soon have no free speech right left at all.[5] Thus, for example, "the effort to defend freedom for those who choose to create, pose for, or view pornography is not only freedom for this particular type of expression but also freedom of expression in general."[6] In *Speaking of Race,*

Speaking of Sex: Hate Speech, Civil Rights, and Civil Liberties, Anthony Griffin and Henry Louis Gates advance positions similar to Strossen's. Gates writes that when the ACLU defended the right of neo-Nazis to march in Skokie, a predominantly Jewish suburb of Chicago where a number of Holocaust survivors lived, it did so to protect and fortify the constitutional right of free speech.[7] If free speech can be tested and upheld to protect even Nazi speech, "then the precedent will make it that much stronger in all the less obnoxious cases."[8] Griffin, who forfeited his position with the Texas NAACP in order to defend a Klan organization, reiterates the ACLU position through a series of three fables, all of which reinforce the notion that the only way to have a strong, vibrant First Amendment is to protect Nazi speech, racist speech, and so on.[9] Otherwise, the periphery will collapse and the government will increasingly regulate speech we regard as central to our system of politics and government.[10]

Enacting hate-speech rules may be evidence of a commitment to democratic dialogue, rather than the opposite.

This type of argument is not just the favorite of the ACLU and its friends. Respected constitutional commentators have employed similar reasoning. Lee Bollinger, for instance, posits that Nazi speech should be protected not because people should value their message in the slightest or believe it should be seriously entertained, but because protection of such speech reinforces our society's commitment to tolerance.[11] Laurence Tribe advances a variant of the same theme. In explaining that there is no principled basis for regulating speech based on content or viewpoint, Tribe states, "If the Constitution forces government to allow people to march, speak, and write in favor or preach brotherhood and justice, then it must also require government to allow them to advocate hatred, racism, and even genocide."[12] As put forward by these and other commentators, then, the "speech we hate" argument takes on a small number of variants. Some argue that there must be a wall around the periphery to protect speech that we hold dear. Others reason that speech that lies at the periphery must be protected if we are to strengthen impulses or principles, such as toleration, that are important to society.

The courts' version

Many years ago, Justice Oliver Wendell Holmes laid the groundwork for the periphery-to-center reasoning by declaring that, "[I]f there is any principle of the Constitution that more imperatively calls for attachment than any other it is the principle of free thought—not the free thought for those who agree with us but freedom for the thought that we hate."[13] He urged that "we should be eternally vigilant against attempts to check even the expression of opinions that we loathe and believe to be fraught with death."[14] Later, in *Brandenburg v. Ohio,* the Supreme Court issued a ringing defense of an unfettered right of free speech. In vindicating the Ku Klux Klan's right to express hatred and violence toward Jews and blacks, the Court held that unless the Klan's speech is likely to incite imminent lawless action, our Constitution has made such speech immune from governmental control.[15] And in the "Nazis in Skokie" case, the Seventh Circuit's opinion reverberated with Justice Holmes's reasoning.[16] In upholding the neo-Nazi's right to march in that city, the court wrote that its result was dictated by the fundamental proposition that if free speech is to remain vital for all, courts must protect not only speech our society deems acceptable, but also that which it justifiably rejects and despises.

Courts, then, make many of the same versions of the core/periphery argument that commentators do: without protection for speech we hate, the free marketplace of ideas will collapse; in order to protect speech that our society finds acceptable we must also protect speech we find repugnant. The argument in each of its guises is essentially the same: to protect the most central, important forms of speech—political and artistic speech, and so on—we must protect the most repugnant, valueless forms including hate speech directed against minorities and degrading pornographic stereotypes of women.

As we mentioned, the extreme-case argument is rarely if ever defended or justified. Rather, its supporters put it forward as an article of faith, without reason or support, as though it were self-evidently true. But is it?

Lack of empirical support

If protecting hate speech and pornography were essential to safeguarding freedom of inquiry and a flourishing democratic politics, we would expect to find that nations that have adopted hate-speech rules and curbs against pornography would suffer a sharp erosion of the spirit of free inquiry. But this has not happened. A host of Western industrialized nations, including Sweden, Italy, Canada, and Great Britain, have instituted laws against hate speech and hate propaganda, many in order to comply with international treaties and conventions requiring such action. Many of these countries have traditions of respect for free speech at least the equal of ours. No such nation has reported any erosion of the atmosphere of free speech or debate. At the same time, the United States, which until recently has refused to put such rules into effect, has a less than perfect record of protecting even political speech. We persecuted communists,[17] hounded Hollywood writers out of the country,[18] and harassed and badgered such civil rights leaders as Josephine Baker,[19] Paul Robeson,[20] and W.E.B. DuBois[21] in a campaign of personal and professional smears that ruined their reputations and denied them the ability to make a living. In recent times, conservatives inside and outside the Administration have disparaged progressives to the point where many are now afraid to use the "liberal" word to describe themselves.[22] Controversial artists are denied federal funding.[23] Museum exhibits that depict the A-bombing of Hiroshima have been ordered modified.[24] If political speech lies at the center of the First Amendment, its protection seems to be largely independent of what is taking place at the periphery. There may, indeed, be an inverse correlation. Those institutions most concerned with social fairness have proved to be the ones most likely to promulgate anti-hate-speech rules. Part of the reason seems to be recognition that hate speech can easily silence and demoralize its victims, discouraging them from participating in the life of the institution.[25] If so, enacting hate-speech rules may be evidence of a commitment to democratic dialogue, rather than the opposite, as some of their opponents maintain.

A paradoxical metaphor

A second reason why we ought to distrust the core-periphery argument is that it rests on a paradoxical metaphor that its proponents rarely if ever explain or justify. Suppose, for example, that one were in the business of supplying electricity to a region. One has competitors—private utility companies, suppliers of gas heaters, and so on. Ninety-nine percent of one's business consists of supplying electricity to homes and businesses, but one also supplies a small amount of electricity to teenagers to recharge the batteries of their Walkmans. It would surely be a strange business decision to focus all or much of one's advertising campaign on the much smaller account. Or take a more legal example. Protecting human security is surely a core value for the police. Yet, it would be a peculiar distribution of police services if a police chief were to reason: human life is the core value which we aim to protect; therefore, we will devote the largest proportion of our resources toward apprehending shoplifters and loiterers.

[Protecting hate speech] draws on a social good to justify an evil deemed only individual, but which in fact is concerted and societywide.

There are situations in which the core-periphery argument does make sense. Providing military defense of a territory may be one; ecology, where protecting lizards may be necessary in order to protect hawks, may be another. But ordinarily the suggestion that to protect a value or thing at its most extreme reaches is necessary in order to protect it at its core requires, at the very least, an explanation. Defenders of hate speech who deploy this argument have not provided one.[26] And, in the meantime, a specious argument does great harm. It treats in grand, exalted terms the harm of suppressing racist speech, drawing illegitimate support from the broad social justification—social dialogue among citizens.[27] The harm to hate speech's victims, out on the periphery, by contrast is treated atomistically, as though it were an isolated event, a mere one-time-only affront to feelings.[28] An injury characterized in act-utilitarian terms obviously cannot trump one couched in broad rule-utilitarian terms.[29] The Nazi derives a halo effect from other, quite legitimate and valuable cases of speech, while the black is seen as a lone, quirky grievant with hypersensitive feelings. But, in reality, hate speech is part of a concerted set of headwinds including many other cases of such speech, that this particular African American victim will experience over the course of his or her life. If we are willing to defend speech in broad social terms, we should be able to consider systemic, concerted harms as well.

The speech-we-hate argument draws plausibility only by ignoring this symmetry. It draws on a social good to justify an evil deemed only individual, but which in fact is concerted and societywide. The unfairness of collapsing the periphery and the center as absolutists do would be made clear if we rendered the argument: "We protect the speech *they* hate in order to protect that which we love." But not only is the argument unfair in this sense, it ignores what makes hate speech peripheral *as speech* in the first place. Face-to-face hate speech—slurs, insults, put-downs, and epithets—are not referential. The recipient learns nothing new about himself or herself.[30] Rather, they are more like performatives, relocating the speaker and victim in social reality. Hate speech is not about the real, but the hyperreal; a Willie Horton ad is like an ad about jeans that makes no factual claim but merely shows a woman and a car.[31]

Mistaking principles for people

There is one setting in which it does make good sense to argue from the extreme or peripheral case, namely where human beings, as opposed to abstract principles, are concerned. For example, one sometimes hears it said that the test of a civilized society is the degree of protection it affords its least privileged, most despised members. Thus prison reformers argue that a society that locks up and warehouses prisoners under crowded and inhumane conditions with little opportunity for recreation, acquisition of jobs skills, or rehabilitation is not deserving of the term "civilized." And so with treatment of the mentally ill, juvenile offenders, the mentally retarded, and the desperately poor. Here, what we do at the periphery does say something about the way society values things like compassion, forgiveness, and the fair distribution of resources. But people, unlike abstract principles, retain their value and distinctive nature even at the furthest reaches. Human beings are always ends in themselves—there is no continuum of humanness.[32] But our constitutional system recognizes not one, but many values.[33] As we shall show, we cannot treat principles, not even the First Amendment, in that fashion.

Face-to-face hate speech—slurs, put-downs, and epithets—are not referential.

Every periphery is another principle's core; that is the nature of a multivalent constitutional system like ours. Principles limit other ones: X's right to privacy limits Y's right to freedom of action, and so on. Indeed, the idea of a constitutional principle, like free speech, that has a core and a periphery would be incoherent without the existence of other values (such as privacy or reputation) to generate the limit that accounts for the periphery. Thus commercial and defamatory speech, which have a lesser degree of constitutional protection than political speech, are subject to limits not because they are not speech at all but because they implicate other values that we hold.[34] And the same is true of speech that constitutes a threat, provokes a fight, defrauds customers, or divulges an official secret. All these and dozens of other "exceptions" to the First Amendment are peripheral, and subject to limits, precisely because they reflect other principles, such as security, reputation, peace, and privacy.[35]

To argue, then, that speech must be protected at the extremest case even more assiduously than when its central values are at stake is either to misunderstand the nature of a constitutional continuum, or to argue that the Constitution in effect has only one value.

Moreover, to argue in such fashion is to violate a principle that is inherent in our constitutional structure and jurisprudence: the principle of dialogic politics.[36] Law has not one value, but many. The district attorney wants the ability to protect the community from offenders; all citizens have an interest in not being randomly seized, frisked, and searched. A wants to speak. B does not wish to be defamed. In situations of competing values, judges attempt to "balance" the principles, trying to fashion a solution that gives the appropriate weight to each.[37] They are guided by lawyers and briefs arguing both sides of the case, as well as case law showing how rights have been balanced in previous decisions. Inherent in this process is what we call dialogic politics, the notion that in cases where interests and values conflict, people and principles (through their defenders, to be sure) ought to be made to talk to each other. In close cases, judges ought to heed both sides; lawyers representing polar views ought to be made to respond to each other's arguments.

But the totalist view admits of no compromise: one's favorite principle remains supreme everywhere it has a bearing, no matter how slight. This means that one is not obliged to talk to those other persons, not obliged to address those other values. If the whole purpose of the First Amendment is to facilitate a system of dialogue and compromise, this is surely a paradoxical view for a defender of that amendment to be taking.

Every totalist argument is indeterminate because it can easily be countered by an opposite and equally powerful countervailing totalism. To continue with the hate-speech example, imagine that someone (say, the NAACP Legal Defense Fund) argued in the following fashion: (1) equality is a constitutional value; (2) the only way effectively to promote equality is to assure that it is protected everywhere; (3) therefore, whenever equality collides with another value, such as free speech, equality must prevail. "We must protect the equality we hate, as much as that which we hold dear." Now we would have two values, the defenders of which are equally convinced should reign supreme. Each regards the other's periphery as unworthy of protection. To be sure, balancing may be troublesome because it can disguise the political value judgments a judge makes on his or her way to a decision. But totalism is worse—it gives the possessor permission not even to enter the realm of politics at all. At least, balancing encourages the decision-maker to be aware and take account of the various values and interests at stake in a controversy. With totalism, one has no need to compromise or consider the other side. One finds oneself outside the realm of politics, and instead inside that of sheer power.

First Amendment romanticism versus racial reality

With hate speech and pornography, heeding the ACLU's totalist argument introduces special dangers of its own. Hate speech lies at the periphery of the First Amendment, as the proponents of the argument quickly concede. Yet the reason why hate speech does so is that it implicates the interest of another group, minorities, in not being defamed, reviled, stereotyped, insulted, badgered, and harassed. Permitting a society to portray a relatively powerless group in this fashion helps construct a stigma-picture or stereotype according to which its members are lascivious, lazy, carefree, immoral, stupid, and so on. This stereotype guides action, making life much more difficult for minorities in transactions that clearly matter: getting a job, renting an apartment, hailing a cab. But it also diminishes the credibility of minority speakers, inhibiting their ability to have their points of view taken seriously, in politics or anywhere else—surely a result that is at odds with the First Amendment and the marketplace of ideas. This is an inevitable result of treating peripheral regions of a value as entitled to the same weight we afford that value when it is centrally implicated: we convey the impression that those other values—the ones responsible for the continuum in the first place—are of little worth. And when those other values are central to the social construction of a human being or social group, the dangers of undervaluing their interests rise sharply. Their interests are submerged today—in the valuing a court or decision-maker is asked to perform. And they are submerged in the future, because their owners are thereafter the bearers of a stigma, one which means they need not be taken fully into account in future deliberations. Permitting one social group to speak disrespectfully of another habituates and encourages speakers to continue speaking that way in the future. This way of speaking becomes normalized, inscribed in hundreds of plots, narratives, and scripts; it becomes part of culture, what everyone knows. The reader may wish to reflect on changes he or she has surely observed over the last fifteen years or so. During the civil rights era of the sixties and early seventies, African Americans and other minorities were spoken of respectfully. Then, beginning in the late seventies and eighties, racism was spoken in code. Today, however, op-ed columns, letters to the editor, and political speeches deride and blame them outspokenly. Anti-minority sentiment need no longer be spoken in code but is right out in the open. We have changed our social construct of the black from unfortunate victim and brave warrior to welfare leeches, unwed mothers, criminals, and untalented low-IQ affirmative action beneficiaries who take away jobs from more talented and deserving whites. The slur, sneer, ethnic joke, and most especially face-to-face hate speech are the main vehicles that have made this change possible.

The core-periphery argument: why it persists

As we have seen, the extreme case (or core-periphery) argument rests on an unexamined, paradoxical metaphor. It adopts a view of the Constitution and of dialogue that is at odds with the one we hold, and it makes the mistake of treating subordinate principles as though they were people and ends in themselves. It treats the interests of minorities as though they were of little weight, or as fully protected by merely protecting speech, including slurs. It ignores the experience of other Western nations that have instituted hate-speech reforms without untoward consequences. What accounts for this argument's rhetorical attraction and staying power? We believe the principal reason is that hate speech and pornography today do not lie at the periphery of the First Amendment, as the ACLU and other advocates urge, but at its center. In former times, society was much more structured than it is now. Citizens knew their places. Women and blacks understood they were not the equals of white men—the Constitution formally excluded them,[38] and coercive social and legal power reminded them of that if they were ever tempted to step out of line.[39] It was not necessary constantly to reinforce this—an occasional reminder would do.[40] Today, however, the formal mechanisms that maintained status and caste are gone or repealed. All that is left is speech and the social construction of reality. Hate speech has replaced formal slavery, Jim Crow laws, female subjugation, and Japanese internment as means to keep subordinate groups in line. In former times, political speech was indeed the center of the First Amendment. Citizens (white, property-owning males, at any rate) did take a lively interest in politics. They spoke, debated, wrote tracts, corresponded with each other about how the Republic ought to be governed. They did not much speak about whether women were men's equals, should be allowed to hold jobs or vote, whether blacks were the equals of whites, because this was not necessary—the very ideas were practically unthinkable.

> *Other Western nations . . . have instituted hate-speech reforms without untoward consequences.*

Today, the situation is reversed. Few Americans vote, or can even name their representative in Washington.[41] Politics has deteriorated to a once-every-four-years ritual of attack ads, catch phrases, sound bites, and image manicuring.[42] At the same time, however, politics in the sense of jockeying for social position has greatly increased in intensity and virulence. Males are anxious and fearful of advances by women;[43] whites fear crime and vengeful behavior from blacks; and so on.[44] Hate speech today is a central weapon in the struggle by the empowered to maintain their position in the face of formerly subjugated groups clamoring for change. It is a means of disparaging the opposition while depicting one's own resistance to sharing opportunities as principled and just. Formerly, the First Amendment and free speech were used to make small adjustments within a relatively peaceful political order consisting of propertied white males. Now it is used to postpone macroadjustments and power-sharing between that group and others: it is, in short, an instrument of majoritarian identity politics. Nothing in the Constitution (at least in the emerging realist view) requires that hate speech receive protection. But ruling elites are unlikely to relinquish it easily, since it is an effective means of postponing social change.

In the sixties, it was possible to believe Harry Kalven's optimistic hypothesis that gains for blacks stemming from the gallant struggle for civil rights would end up benefiting all of society.[45] It was true for a time, at least, that the hard-won gains by a decade of civil rights struggle did broaden speech, due process, and assembly rights for whites as well as blacks.[46] Today, however, there has been a stunning reversal. Now, the reciprocal injury—inhibition of the right to injure others—has been elevated to a central place in First Amendment jurisprudence. The injury—of being muffled when one would otherwise wish to disparage, terrorize,

or burn a cross on a black family's lawn—is now depicted as a prime constitutional value.[47] The interest convergence between black interests and
broadened rights for whites lasted but a short time. Now, the ACLU de-
fends Aryan supremacists, while maintaining that this is best for minorities, too. Blanket resistance to hate-speech regulations, which many college and university administrators are trying to put into place in order to
advance straightforward institutional interests of their own—preserving
diversity, teaching civility, preventing the loss of black undergraduates to
other schools—generates a great deal of business for the ACLU and similar absolutist organizations. In a sense, the ACLU and conservative bigots
are hand-in-glove. Like criminals and police, they understand each other's method of operation, mentality, and objectives. There is a tacit understanding of how each shall behave, how each shall gain from the
other. Indeed, primarily because the Ku Klux Klan and similar clients are
so *bad,* the ACLU gets to feel romantic and virtuous[48]—and the rest of us,
who despise racism and bigotry, are seen as benighted fools because we
do not understand how the First Amendment really works.

But we do. The bigot is not a stand-in for Tom Paine. The best way to
preserve lizards is not to preserve hawks. Reality is not paradoxical. Sometimes, defending Nazis is simply defending Nazis.

Notes

1. SAMUEL WALKER, IN DEFENSE OF AMERICAN LIBERTIES: A HISTORY OF THE ACLU (1990).

2. SAMUEL WALKER, HATE SPEECH: THE HISTORY OF AN AMERICAN CONTROVERSY (1994), at 20, 165–67.

3. *Id.* at 20-21.

4. *Id.* at 160. For example, the ACLU defended the right of Father Terminiello, a suspended Catholic priest, to give a racist speech in Chicago.
The United States Supreme Court agreed with the ACLU in a landmark
decision, Terminiello v. Chicago, 337 U.S. 1 (1949). Walker writes that
the ACLU and other civil rights groups in the 1960s and 1970s were able
to defend free speech rights of civil rights demonstrators by relying on
Terminiello. Id. at 105–8.

5. Henry Louis Gates et al., *Speaking of Race, Speaking of Sex: Hate Speech, Civil
Rights, and Civil Liberties* (1994), at 212.

6. Nadine Strossen, *A Feminist Critique of "The" Feminist Critique of Pornography,* 79 VA. L. REV. 1099, 1171 (1993).

7. SPEAKING OF RACE, *supra.*

8. *Id.*

9. *Id.* at 257–79.

10. *Id.*

11. Lee C. Bollinger, *The Skokie Legacy: Reflections on an "Easy Case" and Free
Speech Theory,* 80 MICH. L. REV. 617, 629–31 (1982); LEE C. BOLLINGER, THE
TOLERANT SOCIETY, Aryeh Neir, DEFENDING MY ENEMY (1974), (making same
general argument in case of Jews, who are in special need of an unfettered
First Amendment).

12. LAURENCE H. TRIBE, AMERICAN CONSTITUTIONAL LAW, 12–8, at 838 n.17 (2d ed. 1988).

13. United States v. Schwimmer, 279 U.S. 644, 654–55 (1929).

14. Abrams v. United States, 250 U.S. 616, 630 (1919). *See* Schenk v. United States, 249 U.S. 47 (1919).

15. Brandenburg v. Ohio, 395 U.S. 444, 448 (1969). *See also* Community Party v. Subversive Activities Control Bd., 367 U.S. 1, 137 (1961) (Black, J., dissenting) ("freedoms of speech . . . must be accorded to the ideas we hate or sooner or later they will be denied to the ideas we cherish"); Cohen v. California, 403 U.S. 15, 22 (1971) ("even scurrilous speech must receive protection").

16. Collins v. Smith, 578 F.2d 1197 (7th Cir. 1978).

17. *See* Dennis v. United States, 341 U.S. 494 (1951).

18. On the infamous "Hollywood blacklist," and resulting exodus to Mexico and other countries by U.S. writers unable to obtain work, see JOHN COYLEY, REPORT ON BLACKLISTING (1956).

19. Mary L. Dudziak, *Josephine Baker, Racial Protest and the Cold War,* 81 J. AM. HIST. 543 (1994).

20. MARTIN B. DUBERMAN, PAUL ROBESON (1988); SHIRLEY GRAHAM, PAUL ROBESON: CITIZEN OF THE WORLD (1971).

21. GERALD HORNE, BLACK AND RED: W.E.B. DUBOIS AND THE AFRO-AMERICAN RESPONSE TO THE COLD WAR, 1944–1963 (1986).

22. On the recent right-wing barrage that has put liberals on the defensive, see Richard Delgado, *Stark Karst* (Book Review), 93 MICH. L. REV. (1995).

23. On the controversy over the National Endowment for the Arts, which has funded controversial artists like Mapplethorpe, see, *e.g.,* Robert Pear, *Chairwoman Comes "not to bury arts endowment but to praise it,"* DENVER POST, Jan. 27, 1995, at A4.

24. Mike Feinsilber, *A-bomb Exhibit to Shrink,* DENVER POST, Jan. 28, 1995, at A4, col. 2.

25. On the way in which hate speech can do this, see, *e.g.,* chapters 1, 4; Frank Michelman, *Response to Cass Sunstein, in* THE PRICE WE PAY: THE CASE AGAINST HATE SPEECH AND PORNOGRAPHY (Laura Lederer & Richard Delgado eds., Farrar, Straus, & Giroux 1996).

26. For our attempt to provide a number of possibilities, see text *supra.*

27. *See* Thomas Emerson, *Toward a General Theory of the First Amendment,* 72 YALE L.J. 877, 878–86 (1963) (setting out the underlying rationales of the First Amendment).

28. *E.g.,* Nadine Strossen, *Regulating Hate Speech on Campus: A Modest Proposal?,* (terming the effect of hate speech a mere "anxiety" [at 492], "offensive" [at 497], "unpleasant" [at 499], or "harmful" [at 533]).

29. Rule utility justifies rules and principles by reason of the good (or evil) they produce; act utility judges the consequences of individual acts.

30. For example, "Nigger, get off this campus. Go back to Africa" conveys no new information, since the target obviously knows (1) he is African American, (2) his ancestors come from that continent, and (3) some in-

dividuals on campus hate him and wish he were not there.

31. *See, e.g.,* JEAN BAUDRILLARD, SIMULATIONS (1983) (on the real and the hyper-real in linguistic theory).

32. A principle of Kantian and Judeo-Christian ethics holds that human beings are valued not instrumentally—for what they can produce—but because of their value in themselves.

33. For example, privacy, property rights, the exercise of religion, the equal protection of the law, freedom from unreasonable searches and seizures, and from being enslaved.

34. *See, e.g.,* LAURENCE H. TRIBE, AMERICAN CONSTITUTIONAL LAW, *supra* at 861-86, 890–904, 931–34, 1046–47.

35. On these so-called exceptions, see chapter 4, this volume [Richard Delgado and Jean Stefancic, *Must We Defend Nazis?* New York: New York University Press, 1997].

36. The term is our own. But it reflects the underlying values of neorepublicanism, the idea that deliberation by the citizenry lies at the heart of our system of law and politics. *See, e.g.,* Frank Michelman, *Law's Republic,* 97 YALE L.J. 1493 (1988); Cass Sunstein, *Beyond the Republican Revival,* 97 YALE L.J. 1539 (1988); Suzanna Sherry, *Civic Virtue and the Feminine Voice in Constitutional Adjudication,* 72 VA. L. REV. 543 (1986). Although a powerful political idea, neorepublicanism is not without its defects; see Richard Delgado, *Rodrigo's Fifth Chronicle: Civitas, Civil Wrongs, and the Politics of Denial,* 45 STAN. L. REV. 1581 (1993).

37. On the ubiquitous balancing test and its appearance in many areas of constitutional law, see AMERICAN CONSTITUTIONAL LAW, *supra,* at 457, 789–94, 944–55, 987, 1037–39, 1251–55.

38. *See* DERRICK BELL, RACE, RACISM, AND AMERICAN LAW 26-30 (3d ed. 1993).

39. *Id.* at 30–36.

40. It was not necessary, in other words, to beat, threaten, or lynch every African American. Only an occasional such act was necessary, because every black knew of the system that supported or winked at such terroristic acts, and was thus constantly aware that he or she could easily become the next victim if he or she committed what the system considered a transgression.

41. On Americans' striking ignorance of Washington and national politics, see, *e.g.,* JAMES FISKLIN, DEMOCRACY AND DELIBERATION 57–64 (1991).

42. *Id.* at 63. *See also* PHYLLIS KANISE, MAKING LOCAL NEWS 110 (1990).

43. SUSAN FALUDI, BACKLASH (1990).

44. *E.g.,* Richard Delgado, *Rodrigo's Eighth Chronicle: Black Crime, White Fears: On the Social Construction of Threat,* 80 VA. L. REV. 503 (1994).

45. HARRY KALVEN, THE NEGRO AND THE FIRST AMENDMENT (1965) (arguing that civil rights gains would benefit all of society, including whites).

46. For example, Goss v. Lopez, 419 U.S. 565 (1975), strengthened due process rights in school disciplinary cases for all students, black or white; a host of cases assured the rights of peaceable assembly and protest [*e.g.,* RACE, RACISM, *supra,* at 424–43 (chapter 6, on rights of political protest)], and so on.

47. *See* R.A.V. v. City of St. Paul, Minnesota, 112 S. Ct. 2538, 2564–65 (1992) (Stevens, J., dissenting) (warning that the majority's opinion has turned First Amendment law on its head—fighting words that were once entirely unprotected are now entitled to greater protection than commercial, and possibly core political, speech).

48. *See* STEVE SHIFFRIN, THE FIRST AMENDMENT, DEMOCRACY, AND ROMANCE (1990) (First Amendment as romance). For a notable example of celebratory First Amendment jurisprudence, see ANTHONY LEWIS, MAKE NO LAW: THE SULLIVAN CASE AND THE FIRST AMENDMENT (1991).

8

Hate Speech Is Protected by the First Amendment

James B. Jacobs and Kimberly Potter

James B. Jacobs is the director of New York University's Center for Research in Crime and Justice and a law professor at NYU School of Law. Kimberly Potter, a former senior research fellow at NYU's Center for Research in Crime and Justice, is a lawyer in private practice in New York. Jacobs and Potter are the authors of Hate Crimes: Criminal Law and Identity Politics.

Prejudiced and demeaning assertions about a person or group's race, color, national origin, religion, gender, sexual orientation, or disability is called hate speech. Unsurprisingly, efforts to outlaw hate speech have been repeatedly problematic and unsuccessful. The ideas upon which anti–hate speech laws and codes are based—hatred and prejudice—are too vague to be meaningful, especially in courts of law. Furthermore, all forms of speech, no matter how provocative, offensive, or demeaning, are equally protected by the First Amendment. Banning "offensive" expression such as hate speech threatens this inalienable right.

The first step in analyzing the constitutionality of hate crime laws is a review of the historic controversy over criminal prohibitions on hate *speech*. Hate speech laws, like hate crime laws, seek to punish and prevent various types of opinions and expressions that the majority deems odious and harmful. Until well into the twentieth century, there was a great deal of judicial uncertainty about whether such prohibitions could pass First Amendment scrutiny.

The impulse to ban "offensive" speech runs deep in every society. The prohibitionist always acts in the name of a higher goal—patriotism, national security, decency, family values, equality, social harmony. While the First Amendment provides unique tolerance for all forms of speech, especially political speech,[1] our history is punctuated with legislative initiatives to ban expression that the majority considers odious—radical ideas, communism, sexually explicit art, flag burning, and group libel, to name just a few. History has not treated these efforts kindly. We now look back on them as irrational and hysterical, as serious affronts to civil rights, and as blights on our commitment to civil liberties.[2]

Fighting words

Of the limited exceptions to the First Amendment protection of expression, "fighting words" is most relevant to our subject. For a short time in American constitutional history, it appeared that a fighting words exception to the First Amendment might provide justification for the suppression of certain forms of hate speech. A half century ago, Walter Chaplinksy, a Jehovah's Witness, called a police officer "a God-damned racketeer," and "a damned Fascist." He was convicted under a New Hampshire law that made it a crime to "address any offensive, derisive or annoying word to any person who is lawfully in any street or other public place, nor call him by any offensive or derisive name." The U.S. Supreme Court rejected Chaplinsky's appeal and carved out a "fighting words" exception to the First Amendment.[3] The Court held that words "which by their very utterance inflict injury or tend to incite an immediate breach of the peace"[4] are not constitutionally protected. The *Chaplinsky* opinion seemingly opened the door to laws prohibiting the utterance of racial, religious, or ethnic insults, because arguably they would "by their very utterance inflict injury." However, in the years after *Chaplinsky*, the Court narrowed the definition of fighting words to utterances *tending to incite an immediate breach of the peace.* Further, the Court stated that in order to constitute "fighting words," the words must "naturally tend to provoke violent resentment" or an "immediate breach of the peace" and must be directed at an individual, rather than at a general group.[5] The Court defined "immediate breach of the peace" to mean more than a mere offensive remark or a breach of decorum; to be legally punishable, the words had to tend to incite the addressee to violent action.[6]

Remarkably, since *Chaplinsky*, the Supreme Court has *never* sustained a conviction under the fighting words doctrine.[7] In other words, every time a state or local government has sought to use criminal law to punish someone for offensive speech that might provoke violent retaliation, the Court has ruled against the government and reversed the conviction. This pattern has led constitutional scholars to doubt the continuing validity of the fighting words exception. As the eminent constitutional scholar, Professor Gerald Gunther, has observed: "one must wonder about the strength of an exception which, while theoretically recognized, has ever since 1942 not been found to be apt in practice."[8]

Group libel

There have been numerous efforts over the course of our history to make it illegal to vilify racial or religious groups; in other words, to engage in what might be called "group libel." Early efforts to ban hate speech emerged during the 1930s in response to perceived Nazi threats. Conflicts between pro- and anti-Nazi groups frequently erupted into violence. According to Professor Samuel Walker, these conflicts produced many anti-expression laws, prohibiting meetings, demonstrations, and distribution of literature.[9] Sometimes called "race hate" or "group libel" laws, they forbade the screening of pro-Fascist films and the distribution of Fascist literature. Other laws banned picketing, parades, demonstrations, and the wearing of uniforms.

In the late 1930s, speech restrictions targeted the distribution of literature and door-to-door solicitation by Jehovah's Witnesses, who were punished for aggressive proselytizing and condemning other religions as "imposters" and "racketeers."[10] Ultimately, however, these laws were struck down as unconstitutional under the First Amendment.[11]

In 1934, in the wake of riots between Nazi sympathizers and anti-Nazi groups, New Jersey passed a group libel law, which outlawed racial and religious "propaganda." The law, premised on the idea that the preservation of liberty and equality required and justified restrictions on those who threaten liberty and equality,[12] provided criminal penalties for dissemination of "propaganda or statements creating or tending to create prejudice, hostility, hatred, ridicule, disgrace or contempt of people . . . by reason of their race, color, creed or manner of worship." It also made it criminal for two or more people to meet and exhibit such propaganda in public or private. For six years, there was not a single prosecution. In 1940, Nazi sympathizers and members of the German-American Bund were convicted of possession of race hate propaganda under the state group libel law. In *State v. Klapprott,*[13] the New Jersey Supreme Court overturned these convictions and declared the group libel law unconstitutional. The court held that the terms "hatred," "prejudice," "hostility," and "abuse" were so vague as to be virtually meaningless. According to the New Jersey court, in the realms of religion and politics there are inevitably strong feelings and sharp differences, including exaggeration, vilification, and false statements. Such expressions, however offensive, are entitled to First Amendment protection, which "in the long view, [is] essential to enlightened opinion and right conduct on the part of the citizens of a democracy."[14]

> *Hate speech laws, like hate crime laws, seek to punish and prevent various types of opinions and expressions that the majority deems odious and harmful.*

The U.S. Supreme Court's modern First Amendment jurisprudence regarding group libel emerged after World War II.[15] The Court's first step was a false start, which for the last time condoned the prohibition of a kind of group libel. In 1952, the Supreme Court heard *Beauharnais v. Illinois,*[16] a challenge to a 1917 Illinois law that made it a crime for anyone "to manufacture, sell, or offer for sale, advertise or publish, present or exhibit in any public place . . . [anything that] portrays depravity, criminality, unchastity, or lack of virtue of a class of citizens, of any race, color, creed, or religion," when such expression would expose such citizens "to contempt, derision, or obloquy or which is productive of breach of the peace or riots."[17] The defendant, Joseph Beauharnais, was the president of the White Circle League of America, a group that had formed in response to the racial integration of some all-white Chicago neighborhoods. White resistance to integration included discrimination by realtors and financial institutions, as well as threats, vandalism, and violence. Beauharnais's literature claimed that whites were threatened by the "rapes, robberies, knives, guns and marijuana of the Negro," and exhorted local government to "halt further encroachment, harassment and invasion of white people, their property, neighborhoods and persons by the Negro." He urged people to petition the government to stop integration. For this bigoted expression, he was charged and convicted.

Expressions, however offensive, are entitled to First Amendment protection.

The U.S. Supreme Court, rather than treating the case as a test of the fighting words doctrine (arguably racially inflammatory literature could trigger immediate violence), took the opportunity to consider whether there was a group libel exception to the First Amendment. In a 5-4 decision, the Court held that the civil unrest and riots in Chicago justified criminal penalties for offensive hate literature that posed a threat to public order. "[T]he willful purveyors of falsehood concerning racial and religious groups promote strife and tend powerfully to obstruct the manifold adjustments required for free, ordered life in a metropolitan, polyglot community."[18] However, Justice William O. Douglas's dissent provided a defense of free expression that later came to prevail:

> Today a white man stands convicted for protesting in unseemly language against our decisions invalidating restrictive [housing] covenants. . . . Tomorrow a Negro [may] be hailed before a court for denouncing lynch law in heated terms.[19]

While the Supreme Court has never explicitly overruled *Beauharnais,* subsequent opinions cast a pall over that ruling, and recognize that the First Amendment protects even the expression of vile prejudices against groups.[20] The landmark case of the modern era is *New York Times v. Sullivan,*[21] which involved a libel claim by an Alabama sheriff against the New York Times for publishing a political advertisement placed by a civil rights group. The advertisement charged Alabama officials with terrorizing and assaulting civil rights demonstrators. The Court held that the statements made in the advertisement were protected by the First Amendment, and that in order to prevail in a libel suit against a particular public figure, a plaintiff has to prove that the statement was "knowingly false or made with reckless disregard for the truth." Indeed, *New York Times v. Sullivan,* effectively sapped the *Beauharnais* group libel rationale of its vitality, by requiring that an individual bringing a libel suit prove the libelous statement was directed *at the individual,* personally, *and not simply at a group to which the individual belongs.*

Even in the case of individual libel, the "knowingly false" test is extremely difficult to satisfy, especially when politics or ideology is involved, as in hate speech cases. For example, statements like "the mayor is a white supremacist, who enjoys oppressing minorities," "Republicans are women-hating Fascists," or "Louis Farrakhan is a racist" would be constitutionally protected regardless of their truth or falsity. Because the First Amendment does not permit the federal government or the states to enshrine certain ideas and beliefs at the expense of others, there can be no law prohibiting an offensive idea.

The Seventh Circuit's famous decision in *Collin v. Smith*[22] poignantly illustrates the First Amendment's protection of expressions of prejudice or hate against groups. Faced with a pending march by a group of Nazis through a predominantly Jewish suburb where approximately 5,000 Holocaust survivors lived, Skokie (Illinois) lawmakers sought to block the Nazis via an ordinance explicitly modeled after the Illinois law upheld in *Beauharnais*. Skokie's ordinance provided that a parade permit could be issued only if a town official determined that the parade

> would not portray criminality, depravity, or lack of virtue in, or incite violence, hatred, abuse or hostility toward a person or group of persons by reason of reference to religious, racial, ethnic, national or regional affiliation.[23]

The Seventh Circuit held the Skokie ordinance unconstitutional because it sought to regulate speech based on its content. The court also said that the ban on the Nazis could not be justified as a prohibition against fighting words. While acknowledging that the Nazi march would be offensive and painful to the town's Jewish residents, especially the Holocaust survivors, the court stated that such anguish is the price we pay for free speech.

> [W]e think the words of the [Supreme] Court in *Street v. New York* [394 U.S. 576, 592 (1969)] are very much on point: "Any shock effect . . . must be attributed to the content of the ideas expressed. It is firmly settled that under our Constitution the public expression of ideas may not be prohibited merely because the ideas are themselves offensive to some of their hearers."[24]

Referring to *Beauharnais,* the court noted that the Skokie ordinance could not be upheld simply on the basis of "blind obeisance to uncertain implications from an opinion issued years before the Supreme Court itself rewrote the rules." The Supreme Court denied Skokie's petition for *certiorari,* letting the Seventh Circuit's opinion stand. Today, even if riots were threatened, the First Amendment would protect offensive racist, anti-Semitic, anti-ethnic literature and expression because "[i]f there is a bedrock principle underlying the First Amendment, it is that the government may not prohibit the expression of an idea simply because society finds it offensive or disagreeable."[25]

Campus speech codes

By the late 1950s, group libel laws had fallen out of favor. Professor Walker attributes this trend primarily to the lack of support for such laws from civil rights and religious groups who were their putative beneficiaries.

> [I]t is the lack of an effective advocate that accounts for the

failure of hate speech restrictions to gain any ground in the United States. . . . The major civil rights groups came to understand that any exception to the seamless fabric of individual rights, which group libel represented, threatened the entire structure. One critical element of the civil rights movement, which had direct ramifications for the hate speech issue, was that activity on behalf of racial equality often involved provocative and offensive tactics by civil rights groups themselves.[26]

In the late 1980s, efforts to restrict hate speech surfaced again, this time in the form of college and university disciplinary codes outlawing bigoted expressions.[27] Proponents of these university-sponsored codes claim that prejudiced and bigoted speech injures members of minority groups and undermines minority students' ability to fulfill their academic potential. According to the proponents, "from the victim's perspective racist hate messages cause real damage"[28]; "we have not listened to the real victims—we have shown so little understanding of their injury."[29] They argue that racist, anti-Semitic, misogynistic, and homophobic expressions and epithets inflict emotional and psychological injury on the individual and on members of the group to which the individual belongs. Professor Mari Matsuda, a leading proponent of hate speech codes, asserts that,

> [r]acist speech is best treated as a *sui generis* category, presenting an idea so historically untenable, so dangerous, and so tied to perpetuation of violence and degradation of the very classes of human beings who are least equipped to respond that it is properly treated as outside the realm of protected discourse.[30]

Campus hate speech codes have not fared well in court. All three constitutional challenges have been successful.[31] *Doe v. University of Michigan*[32] involved the University of Michigan's "Policy on Discrimination and Discriminatory Harassment of Students" which prohibited and punished *any* behavior that had the effect of "stigmatizing and victimizing individuals on the basis of race, ethnicity, religion, sex, sexual orientation, creed, national origin, ancestry, age, marital status, handicap or Vietnam-era veteran status."[33] An interpretive guide illuminated the types of expression subject to sanctions. Some examples included:

- A male student makes remarks in class like "Women just aren't as good in this field as men," thus creating a hostile learning atmosphere for female classmates.

- Students in a residence hall have a floor party and invite everyone on their floor except one person because they think she is a lesbian.[34]

The second example is curious because it does not involve expression. The interpretive guide also cited examples of harassment such as "telling jokes about homosexuals," sponsoring "entertainment that includes a comedian who slurs Hispanics," displaying a confederate flag in a private dorm room, laughing at jokes "about someone in your class who stutters."[35]

The federal district court held that the university's policy was unconstitutionally vague because it "swept within its scope a significant amount of 'verbal conduct' or 'verbal behavior' which is unquestionably protected speech under the First Amendment."[36] As to the issue of vagueness, the court held that "[l]ooking at the plain language of the Policy, it was simply impossible to discern any limitation on its scope or any conceptual distinction between protected and unprotected conduct." Although the university insisted that it had not applied the policy to protected speech, the court pointed to several students against whom disciplinary charges had been brought, despite their having engaged only in constitutionally protected speech. In one case, a complaint was filed against a graduate student who, during a class discussion, said that homosexuality was a disease and that he intended to develop a counseling plan to return gays to heterosexuality. Other instances involved (1) during a class public speaking exercise, a student read "an allegedly homophobic limerick which ridiculed a well known athlete for his presumed sexual orientation"; and (2) a student complained that "he had heard that minorities had a difficult time in [a dentistry] course . . . and that they were not treated fairly" by the minority professor. Both students "plea bargained," agreeing to "counseling." The student who read the limerick attended an "educational gay rap session" and wrote a letter of apology, which was published in the university newspaper. After being "counseled," the student who complained about the dentistry class agreed to write a letter apologizing for making the comment without adequately verifying the allegation.[37] The court observed that:

> The Administrator generally failed to consider whether a comment was protected by the First Amendment before informing the accused student that a complaint had been filed. The Administrator instead attempted to persuade the accused student to accept "voluntary" sanctions. Behind this persuasion was, of course, the subtle threat that failure to accept such sanctions might result in a formal hearing. There is no evidence in the record that the Administrator ever declined to pursue a complaint . . . because the alleged harassing conduct was protected by the First Amendment.[38]

In *UWM Post, Inc. v. Board of Regents of the University of Wisconsin,*[39] a federal court heard a challenge to a university policy that provided sanctions for "racist or discriminatory comments, epithets or other expressive behavior . . . [that] demean[s] the race, sex, religion, color, creed, disability, sexual orientation, national origin, ancestry or age of the individual or individuals; and creates an intimidating, hostile, or demeaning environment."[40] The university had relied upon the policy to punish:

- A student who called another student "Shakazulu."
- A student who shouted "fucking bitch" and "fucking cunt" at a woman because of her negative statements in the university's paper about the athletic department.
- A student who told an Asian student that "it's people like you— that's the reason this country is screwed up. You don't belong here. Whites are always getting screwed by minorities and some day the Whites will take over."

- A student who, during an argument, called another student "a fat-ass nigger."
- A student who yelled at a female student "you've got nice tits."[41]

While acknowledging the offensiveness of these comments, the court found the policy unconstitutionally overbroad and vague. The court rejected the university's claim that the policy prohibited only fighting words. "Since the elements of the [policy] do not require that the regulated speech, by its very utterance, tend to incite violent reaction, the rule goes beyond the present scope of the fighting words doctrine."[42] Further, "[i]t is unlikely that all or nearly all demeaning, expressive behavior which creates an intimidating, hostile or demeaning environment tends to provoke a violent response."[43]

It is unlikely that all or nearly all demeaning, expressive behavior which creates an intimidating, hostile or demeaning environment tends to provoke a violent response.

In striking down UWM's speech code, the court relied upon the Seventh Circuit's decision in *Hudnut v. American Booksellers Association, Inc.*[44] (summarily affirmed by the Supreme Court).[45] *Hudnut* involved a First Amendment challenge to an Indianapolis ordinance which (1) prohibited the production, distribution, exhibition, or sale of pornography and the display of pornography in any place of employment, school, public place, or private home; (2) created a civil cause of action for persons coerced, intimidated, or tricked into appearing in a pornographic work; and (3) provided victims of sexual violence a cause of action against sellers of the pornography. The ordinance was premised on the city council's finding that:

> Pornography is a systematic practice of exploitation and subordination based on sex which differentially harms women. The bigotry and contempt it promotes, with the acts of aggression it fosters, harms women's opportunities for equality of rights in employment, education, access to and use of public accommodations, and acquisition of real property; promotes rape, battery, child abuse, kidnapping and prostitution . . . ; and contributes significantly to restricting women in particular from full exercise of citizenship and participation in public life.[46]

The Seventh Circuit held that Indianapolis's definition of pornography—"the graphic sexually explicit subordination of women"—was impermissibly vague and overbroad. The Court of Appeals rejected the city's argument that the ordinance banned only speech that had a socially "low value." According to Judge Frank Easterbrook, the ordinance created an impermissible "approved view of women, of how they may react to sexual encounters [and] of how the sexes may relate to each other."[47]

Commenting on the *Hudnut* case, Harvard Law School professor Laurence Tribe stated,

[T]he First Amendment similarly protects advocacy . . . of the opinion that women were meant to be dominated by men, or blacks to be dominated by whites, or Jews by Christians, and that those so subordinated not only deserve but subconsciously enjoy their humiliating treatment. . . . It is an inadequate response to argue, as do some scholars, that ordinances like that enacted by Indianapolis take aim at harms, not at expression. *All* viewpoint-based regulations are targeted at some supposed harm.[48]

In summary, under existing First Amendment jurisprudence, hate *speech* cannot be prohibited or made illegal.

Notes

1. "International Legal Colloquium on Racial and Religious Hatred and Group Libel," 22 Israel Yearbook on Human Rights 1–259 (1992); N. Lerner, The U.N. Convention on the Elimination of All Forms of Racial Discrimination (2d ed. 1980); United Kingdom Race Relations Act of 1965, ch. 73 § 6(1) (amended in 1976 and 1986); J. Griffiths, "Conflict in Society: Public Order v. Individual Liberty—Laws Against Incitement to Racial Hatred," paper delivered at Asia Pacific Lawyers Association Third General Assembly, Hawaii, Jan. 6–9, 1989. Canadian court decisions upholding hate speech restrictions include: Regina v. Keegstra, 19 C.C.C. (3d) 254 (Alta. Q.B. 1984), and Regina v. Zundel, 31 C.C.C. (3d) 97, 580 O.R. (2d) 129 (Ont. C.A. 1987).

2. Samuel Walker, Hate Speech: The History of an American Controversy (Lincoln: University of Nebraska Press, 1994).

3. Chaplinsky v. New Hampshire, 315 U.S. 568 (1942).

4. Chaplinsky at 571–72.

5. Gooding v. Wilson, 405 U.S. 518, 524 (1972).

6. Texas v. Johnson, 491 U.S. 397 (1989).

7. Gerald Gunther, Constitutional Law, 12th ed. (Mineola, NY: Foundation Press, 1991), p. 1073.

8. Gerald Gunther, Stanford University Campus Report, May 3, 1989, p. 18.

9. Walker, Hate Speech, p. 40.

10. Ibid., p. 64–65.

11. Lovell v. Griffin, 303 U.S. 444 (1938) (holding unconstitutional a permit requirement for distribution of literature by Jehovah's Witnesses); Martin v. Struthers, 319 U.S. 141 (1943) (upholding First Amendment right of Jehovah's Witnesses to solicit door-to-door); Cantwell v. Connecticut, 310 U.S. 296 (1940) (holding unconstitutional criminal conviction of a Jehovah's Witness based on offensive speech).

12. Walker, Hate Speech, p. 55.

13. 22 A.2d 877 (1941).

14. Klapprott at 877.

15. Floyd Abrams, "Hate Speech: An American View, Group Libel and Criminal Law: Walking on the 'Slippery Slope,'" 22 Israel Yearbook on Human

Rights 85 (1992); Natan Lerner, "Incitement in the Racial Convention: Reach and Shortcomings of Article 4," 22 Israeli Yearbook on Human Rights 1 (1992); Kenneth Lasson, "Group Libel v. Free Speech, When Big Brother Should Butt In," 23 Duquesne Law Review 77 (1984).

16. 343 U.S. 250 (1952).

17. Beauharnais at 250.

18. Id.

19. Id.

20. Laurence Tribe, American Constitutional Law, 2d ed. (Mineola, NY: Foundation Press, 1988), p. 926; Gerald Gunther, Constitutional Law, 11th ed. (Mineola, NY: Foundation Press, 1985), p. 1055.

21. 376 U.S. 254 (1964).

22. 578 F.2d 1197 (7th Cir. 1978).

23. Collin v. Smith at 1199.

24. Id. at 1206.

25. Texas v. Johnson, 491 U.S. 397, 414 (1989).

26. Walker, Hate Speech, p. 78.

27. Milton Heumann & Thomas W. Church, with David Redlawsk, Hate Speech on Campus: Cases, Case Studies, and Commentary (Boston: Northeastern University Press, 1997); Robert M. O'Neil, Free Speech in the College Community (Bloomington: University of Indiana Press, 1997).

28. Mari Matsuda, "Public Response to Racist Speech: Considering the Victim's Story," 87 Michigan Law Review 2320, 2340 (August 1989).

29. Charles R. Lawrence, III, "If He Hollers Let Him Go: Regulating Racist Speech on Campus," 1990 Duke Law Journal 431, 436 (1990).

30. Matsuda, "Public Response to Racist Speech," p. 2357.

31. Doe v. University of Michigan, 721 F. Supp. 852 (E.D. Mich. 1989); UWM Post v. Board of Regents of the University of Wisconsin, 774 F. Supp. 1163 (E.D. Wis. 1991); Dambrot v. Central Michigan University, 839 F. Supp. 477 (E.D. Mich. 1993).

32. 721 F. Supp. 852 (E.D. Mich. 1989). See also UWM Post v. Board of Regents of the University of Wisconsin, 774 F. Supp. 1163 (E.D. Wis. 1991) (declaring unconstitutional campus hate speech code).

33. Doe at 853.

34. Id. at 858.

35. Id.

36. Id. at 853.

37. Id. at 866.

38. Id.

39. 774 F. Supp. 1163 (E.D. Wis. 1991).

40. UWM Post at 1165.

41. Id. at 1167–68.

42. Id. at 1172.
43. Id. at 1173.
44. 771 F.2d 323 (7th Cir. 1985).
45. 106 S.Ct. 1172 (1986).
46. Code of Indianapolis and Marion County, Indiana, § 16–1(a) (2).
47. Hudnut at 328.
48. Tribe, American Constitutional Law, p. 925 (emphasis in original).

9

Many Crimes Against Gays Are Hate Crimes

Human Rights Campaign

The Human Rights Campaign (HRC) is a nonprofit organization dedicated to ending discrimination against lesbian, gay, bisexual, and transgendered Americans. The campaign sponsors the National Coming Out Project.

A growing number of Americans are targeted by crimes motivated by real or perceived differences in sexual orientation. Today, the FBI claims that sexual orientation–based offenses are the third most commonly reported hate crimes. Often these attacks are especially brutal, intended to send a message to gay, lesbian, bisexual, and transgendered communities that "their kind" will not be tolerated. However, the federal government only investigates hate crimes involving race, color, religion, and national origin. Because hate crimes based on sexual orientation are a serious national problem, current hate crime laws need to be enhanced so that every hate crime victim can seek federal assistance.

Lesbian, gay and bisexual Americans are frequent targets of vicious hate crimes. Only in rare circumstances, however, can the federal government help in investigating and prosecuting hate crimes committed against someone because of his or her real or perceived sexual orientation. Thus, federal law enforcement authorities cannot assist in anti-gay hate crimes—as they do in hate crimes based on race, color, religion or national origin. The Human Rights Campaign (HRC) advocates for adding actual or perceived gender, sexual orientation and disability to laws governing prosecution of hate crimes. HRC believes that hate crimes based on sexual orientation should be investigated and prosecuted on an equal basis as other categories of hate crimes now covered by state and federal law.

All violent crimes are reprehensible. But the damage done by hate crimes cannot be measured solely in terms of physical injury or dollars and cents. Hate crimes rend the fabric of our society and fragment communities because they target a whole group and not just the individual victim. Hate crimes are committed to make an entire community fearful. A violent hate crime is intended to "send a message" that a person and his or her "kind" will not be tolerated—many times leaving the victim and others in their group feeling isolated, vulnerable and unprotected. Eighty-five percent of law enforcement officials recently surveyed say they recognize this type of violence to be more serious than similar crimes not motivated by bias, according to a study funded by the U.S. Department of Justice's Bureau of Justice Statistics.

Hate crimes [motivated by sexual orientation] are often inordinately severe, sometimes going well beyond the force needed even to kill someone.

Further, statistics support that gay, lesbian, and bisexual Americans are often targeted for violence. Under the Hate Crimes Statistics Act, the Federal Bureau of Investigation consistently reports that hate crimes based on sexual orientation are the third highest reported category of hate crimes— behind race and religion, respectively. The category of sexual orientation is not currently included in any federal criminal civil rights laws. In addition, many gays and lesbians are not "out" to their families, coworkers or friends, and thus they believe they have no one to seek assistance from or even discuss their experience with hate-motivated violence.

Hate crimes are often inordinately severe, sometimes going well beyond the force needed even to kill someone. For example, a gay man died after being stabbed 35 times during a recent hate crime in Texas.

An underreported problem

Law enforcement experts agree that when compared to other crimes, hate crimes are underreported to the police. Minority groups, including gays and lesbians, historically have had strained relations with law enforcement officials and fear what is called "re-victimization," whereby the officials verbally or physically attack the person who reports the crime. They fear that officials also may blame them, and be unwilling to write up a report.

Researchers found that only one-third of victims of anti-gay hate crimes reported the incident to police, as compared to 57 percent of the victims of random crimes, according to a study funded by the National Institute of Mental Health. It found that many victims of anti-gay incidents do not report the crimes to local law enforcement officials because they fear their sexual orientation may be made public—to family, employers and others—or they fear they will receive insensitive or hostile treatment, including physical abuse. The National Bias Crimes Training for Law Enforcement and Victim Assistance Professionals calls this phenomena "secondary injury"—the victim's perceived rejection by, and lack of, expected support from the community.

An example of this occurred as a result of the bombing of the predominantly lesbian bar in Atlanta in February 1997. Five bar patrons were injured severely enough to be taken to the hospital by ambulance. However, one victim who had a shrapnel wound refused to be treated when she saw reporters in the hospital emergency room.

In addition, people are less motivated to report hate crimes to authorities in those jurisdictions where no hate crime laws covering sexual orientation exist. If a perpetrator cannot be prosecuted, victims may consider it a waste of time and energy to report the crime.

Although hate crimes based on sexual orientation are underreported, the number of hate crimes reported suggests an appalling amount of bias-motivated violence against gays and lesbians. As overall serious crime continued to decrease for the eighth consecutive year, hate crimes based on sexual orientation have continued to rise and increased 4.5 percent from 1998 to 1999, according to the FBI's Uniform Crime Reports. Reported hate crime incidents based on sexual orientation have more than tripled since the FBI began collecting statistics in 1991—comprising 16.7 percent of all hate crimes for 1999 at 1,317. Hate crimes based on sexual orientation continue to make up the third highest category after race and religion, which make up 54.5 and 17.9 percent, respectively of the total, 7,876.

Evidence indicates that FBI data does not paint the whole picture, however. The National Coalition of Anti-Violence Programs, a private organization that tracks bias incidents against gay, lesbian, bisexual and transgender people, reported 1,965 incidents in 1999 in 25 cities/jurisdictions across the country while the FBI collected 1,317 incidents from 12,122 reporting agencies for the year.

Current state laws are inadequate

Only 25 states and the District of Columbia now have hate crime laws that include "sexual orientation" in the list of protected categories. Forty-five states have hate crimes laws, but their listing of categories do not all include "sexual orientation." Six states have no hate crimes laws whatsoever.

In May 1997, South Carolina Attorney General Charles Condon drafted a hate crime bill for the state in response to the burning of numerous African-American churches there. The draft bill did not include sexual orientation because, according to Condon's legislative lobbyist, "Nobody has demonstrated to us that there's a problem [with people being attacked because of their sexual orientation], so we decided to take action against race-based hate crimes." However, there were at least four documented reports of anti-gay hate crimes in the state in the previous year. A hate crime victim from South Carolina also testified before the Senate Judiciary Committee in June 1997 about a violent beating that occurred in April 1996 that left him without hearing in one ear, broken ribs, and 47 stitches in his face. The perpetrators yelled, "We're going to get you, faggot," he said. He was left for dead in a trash bin outside a primarily heterosexual bar in Myrtle Beach, S.C.

Federal law is also inadequate

Currently, only two federal hate crime statutes include the category of sexual orientation:

The Hate Crimes Statistics Act (PL 101-275) became law in 1990 and was reauthorized in 1996. This law requires the FBI to collect statistics on hate crimes on the basis of race, religion, ethnicity, sexual orientation and disability. Although the FBI is required to collect and analyze the statistics from local and state law enforcement agencies, the local and state agencies are *not* required to provide statistics to the FBI. This law does not allow federal assistance in investigation and prosecution of hate crimes or enhance penalties for hate crime perpetrators; it simply compiles statistics from the various local and state jurisdictions that report to the FBI.

The number of hate crimes reported suggests an appalling amount of bias-motivated violence against gays and lesbians.

The Hate Crimes Sentencing Enhancement Act (PL 103-322) was passed as a part of the Violent Crime Control and Law Enforcement Act of 1994. This law directs the U.S. Sentencing Commission to provide sentencing enhancements of "not less than three offense levels for offenses that the finder of fact at trial determines beyond a reasonable doubt are hate crimes." This law is considered the federal counterpart to state hate crime penalty statutes, to be used for hate crimes committed on *only* federal property, such as national parks. Because the law can only be used when a crime is perpetrated on federal property, it is very rarely used.

A broad coalition of groups, including 175 civil rights, civic, religious, state and local government associations and law enforcement organizations, supports legislation to amend current federal criminal civil rights law under the Civil Rights Act of 1968 (18 U.S.C. 245). These changes would provide authority for federal officials to investigate and prosecute cases in which the violence occurs because of a victim's actual or perceived gender, sexual orientation and disability, and would eliminate an overly restrictive jurisdictional obstacle to prosecution. This legislation, the Hate Crimes Prevention Act, was originally introduced in 1997 after a White House Conference on Hate Crimes.

Since then, the majority of lawmakers in the U.S. Congress voted in support of the legislation when a revised version, the Local Law Enforcement Enhancement Act, was offered as an amendment to the Senate Department of Defense Authorization bill in June 2000. The bill passed the Senate in a bipartisan vote, 57 to 42, including 13 Republicans. In September 2000, the House passed a motion to instruct in support of the measure, 232 to 192, including 41 Republicans. Despite these strong votes, opponents of the legislation were able to strip the bill from the Defense Department bill before the end of the 106th Congress. The bill was reintroduced in the 107th Congress with a record number of original cosponsors (S. 625/H.R. 1343). HRC supports this bill and will work for its passage.

An important backstop

18 U.S.C. 245 is one of the primary statutes used to combat racial and religious violence. The statute currently prohibits intentional interference with enjoyment of a federal right or benefit, such as attending school or

being employed, on the basis of the victim's race, religion, national origin or color. Under this statute, the government must prove the crime occurred because of the victim's race (or other protected category) and because he or she was enjoying a specifically enumerated federally protected right. These dual requirements have severely restricted the ability of the federal government to act in appropriate cases.

State and local authorities have played, and will continue to play, the primary role in investigating and prosecuting hate violence. But federal jurisdiction would provide an important backstop to ensure that justice is achieved in every case. The Local Law Enforcement Enhancement Act limits the federal government's jurisdiction to only the most serious violent crimes directed at persons, resulting in death or bodily injury, and not property crimes. This measure would allow states with inadequate resources to take advantage of Justice Department resources and personnel in limited cases that have been authorized by the attorney general. And it enables federal, state and local authorities to work together as partners in the investigation and prosecution of bias-related crimes.

10

Anti-Gay Crimes Are Not Hate Crimes

Rosaline Bush

Rosaline Bush is the editor of Family Voice, *a publication of Concerned Women for America (CWA). CWA is a women's organization that promotes Christian values and morality in family life and public policy.*

All violent crimes are filled with hatred. But the murder of college student Matthew Shepard is called a "hate crime" because he was a homosexual. Advocates of homosexuality contend that gays and lesbians are victims of intolerance and want to add sexual orientation to hate crime laws. However, homosexuality is a lifestyle choice and behavior that can be changed, not an "inborn, innate, unchangeable" characteristic. Including sexual orientation in hate crime laws would give homosexuals special treatment and be disastrous for Christians and those who believe homosexuality is immoral.

*A*ir Force Academy cadet David Graham and Annapolis cadet Diana Zamora killed a teenage girl who had sex with David. Both cadets were found guilty of capital murder and sentenced to life imprisonment.
   Brian Stewart didn't want to pay child support. So he injected his 11-month-old son with HIV. Today, the seven-year-old boy is doomed to a slow, tortuous death. Stewart will spend the rest of his life behind bars.
   Aaron McKinney and Russell Henderson allegedly robbed a college student, pistol-whipped him, tied him to a log fence and beat him into unconsciousness. Matthew Shepard died five days later. The prosecutor is seeking execution.
   Were you outraged when you heard about these brutal crimes? Although we hear about violent acts everyday—from child abuse to Christian persecution—it's still hard not to wonder, "What kind of monster could do that to another human being?"
   Murder is as old as time. Cain, spurred by jealous hatred, killed his brother Abel. Now mankind continues to follow in his violent footsteps. David Graham and Diana Zamora hated the girl who came between them. And Brian Stewart hated both his ex-wife and young son.

Reprinted from "Hate Crimes and Punishment," by Rosaline Bush, *Family Voice*, March 1999. Reprinted with permission.

All brutal acts are fueled by hatred. Yet only Aaron McKinney and Russell Henderson have been accused of committing a "hate crime." Why? Because their victim, Matthew Shepard, was a homosexual.

That begs the question: Was Matthew's life worth more than the young girl or more than an innocent infant? For the most part, your answer depends on whether or not you advocate homosexuality. The average Christian was shocked and outraged at the brutality of the criminals who killed Matthew Shepard—but no more so than at a father who would doom his own son to a life of pain and premature death.

"Matthew Shepard's murder is a horrible crime. But Matthew's chosen lifestyle, party affiliation or religion don't alter the brutality of that," said CWA President Carmen Pate. "All crimes are hate crimes."

Homosexuals, emboldened by tremendous support, have pushed for "minority" status.

So what makes Matthew Shepard the poster child for "hate crimes"? Politicians and entertainers in particular have embraced the gay agenda. Today, homosexuality is politically correct. And homosexuals, emboldened by tremendous support, have pushed for "minority" status.

In his State of the Union address in January 1999, President Clinton honored the civil rights activist Rosa Parks. However, he used her noble efforts as a platform for endorsing his homosexual rights agenda—the Employment Non-Discrimination Act (ENDA) and the Hate Crimes Prevention Act.

Indeed, all crimes are motivated by hate. But as Americans, we have always had the right to hold any opinion—however good or bad. Traditionally, courts have only stepped in when crimes have resulted. Hatred toward any group or individual because of race, creed, color or lifestyle choice is wrong. But only God—not legislators—can deal with this problem. He alone knows the motivations of our hearts.

Who gets special treatment?

Many people have suffered genuine bigotry or a loss of their civil rights. In the early history of our country, African Americans were brought to our shores as slaves. The battle for their civil rights culminated in the 1960s when Martin Luther King, Jr., proclaimed his dream of equality among races.

In the mid-nineteenth century, Chinese-Americans were exploited as cheap labor in the mines and on the railroads. And around the time of World War II, Japanese-Americans were forced to relocate in internment camps. Even today, unscrupulous people target ethnic groups that constitute genuine minorities.

To qualify for federal protection under civil rights laws, groups must:
- Prove their characteristic is inborn, innate and unchangeable
- Show they are economically disadvantaged
- Demonstrate they are politically powerless

Homosexuals claim that sexual preference is inborn and unchangeable; yet they cannot provide conclusive medical evidence. Furthermore, thousands of *ex*-gays have proven that homosexuality can be changed. Considering statistics that compare the group to average wage earners, they would also have a difficult time proving economic disadvantage. And to say they have no political clout is ludicrous. Former President Clinton, Hollywood, the media and big business—which have been swayed by homosexual rhetoric—vehemently push their agenda.

As a result of smooth politicking, activists have gained rights—not equal to but—above and beyond the average American. The homosexual community has rallied around "hate crimes" supposedly committed against them. But what exactly is a "hate crime"?

Hate crimes defined

According to the Anti-Defamation League (ADL), a hate crime is any crime committed because of the victim's actual or perceived race, color, religion, ancestry, national origin, disability, gender or *sexual orientation.*" [Our emphasis]

How is hatred becoming the single most important factor in evaluating a crime? Over 50 percent of all "hate crimes" reported by the Justice Department in 1998 involved either intimidation or simple assault. Many did not even include physical touching. Again, what exactly is a "hate crime"?

In mid-December 1998, actor Alec Baldwin appeared on "Late Night with Conan O'Brien." When the NBC host asked about the president's impeachment, Baldwin jumped from his chair, flailed his arms and screamed, *"If we lived in other countries, we would go down to Washington and we would stone Henry Hyde to death. And we would go to their homes and kill their women and their children!"*

Although "tolerance" is their byword, advocates of "hate crimes" legislation promote a zealous *intolerance* for pro-family and religious views on this volatile issue. *Hate-monger, intolerant* and *gay-basher* are favorite labels for anyone opposing them. But who are the intolerant ones?

Who's kidding whom?

If a Christian had spewed threats like Mr. Baldwin, the press would still be broadcasting his "hate speech." However, let's compare Baldwin's outburst to Senator Trent Lott's commentary on the "Armstrong Williams Show" in June. Senator Lott responded to the host's question: "Do you think homosexuality is a sin?" He replied: "Yeah, it is. You should love that person. You should not try to mistreat them or treat them as outcasts. You should try to show them a way to deal with that problem, just like alcohol, or sex addiction or kleptomaniacs."

Predictably, homosexual advocates vilified Lott:

"Lott's mean-spirited pronouncements are part of an escalating pattern of political gay-baiting . . . hate rhetoric from anti-gay extremists and those who pander to them."

—Brian K. Bond, Executive Director, Gay & Lesbian Victory Fund

"Where does this pain, self-hatred and suffering originate? From hateful comments like Senator Lott's."

—C. Ray Drew, Executive Director, Gay & Lesbian Victory Fund

"The ridiculous and hateful statements that Trent Lott made . . . compel them [Americans] to act that homophobia out in the form of violent acts against lesbian, gay, bisexual and transgender people."
—Christine Quinn, Executive Director, New York City Gay and Lesbian Anti-Violence Project.

About the same time as Senator Lott's comments, CWA and other pro-family groups sponsored a series of ads in major newspapers. The "Truth in Love" advertisement campaign was meant to demonstrate love to homosexuals—and hope. We want them to know it is possible to leave their lifestyle.

When Matthew Shepard was murdered, homosexuals used his death as an excuse for blasting conservatives and Christians.

Although many individuals sought help after reading the ads, the homosexual community reacted with vengeance. It accused the "religious right" of inciting hatred and promoting intolerance. They declared that our ads contained rhetoric that "trickled down" into violence against homosexuals. Then when Matthew Shepard was murdered, homosexuals used his death as an excuse for blasting conservatives and Christians. *If the public believes this, why isn't it concerned that Baldwin's outrageous comments might incite mob violence?*

President Clinton has directed Attorney General Janet Reno to make a priority of the "hate crimes" issue. And she has already asked all 93 U.S. Attorneys to appoint federal "hate crime" coordinators. "Hate crimes will not be tolerated," Reno said. President Clinton called for the 105th Congress to pass the proposed federal Hate Crimes Prevention Act quickly before adjourning for the elections. But time ran out; Congress did not pass it.

Meanwhile, the Human Rights Campaign has been working on a bipartisan measure to be introduced in this Congress. They want to amend federal "hate crimes" laws to include *sexual orientation*.

Watch that first step

Adding sexual orientation to this legislation will prove disastrous for people who oppose the homosexual lifestyle on moral grounds. "Hate crime" laws will squelch their voice.

These laws curtail debate on the radical practices that homosexuals are trying to implement, such as same-sex "marriage," lowering the age of consent for boys, and using the public schools to teach homosexual behavior.

Christians, in embracing "tolerance," have not examined the inherent danger in "hate crime" legislation. If speaking out against homosexuality becomes a crime, then merely holding Christian beliefs can become dangerous. Hate crimes legislation is the first step toward making it a crime to preach the Good News.

Sam and Joe each have beaten up innocent victims—but Sam uttered disdain for homosexuals in the process. Therefore, he received a stiffer sentence under a "hate crimes" law. Yet they committed the same crime.

The *Southern Voice,* a newspaper advocating homosexuality said: "[The Shepard murder] is made worse by the prejudiced motive . . . 'Hate crime' laws add to the criminal punishment an additional one that corresponds with the additional interference with the victim's rights."

But as a columnist for the *Boston Globe* stated, "[Criminals] should be punished because of their deeds—not because they are bigots."

"Bigotry and hatred are always wrong," says CWA President Carmen Pate. "But people ought not be punished because of feelings or beliefs. To categorize personal beliefs into *approved* or *disapproved* isn't the role of government."

Prosecuting anyone for their *bigotry*—whether against blacks, whites, Asians, or any other group of individuals—is wrong.

Instead, the government must prosecute only criminal acts resulting from those thoughts. And criminal actions are *already* illegal and prosecutable.

"Hate crimes" legislation is progressive. It began by "protecting" races and has more recently moved on to homosexuals.

No single piece of legislation can eliminate bigotry. You cannot legislate emotions and feelings. CWA wants no part of "hate crimes" legislation, which does *nothing* to stop underlying hatred and does *everything* to take away our freedom of thought and expression.

If "hate crimes" legislation is passed, Christians may be punished for daring to say that homosexuality is wrong. Since we are called to speak the truth in love, can we take the chance of being permanently silenced?

11

It's a Crime: Will Gender Be Included in Federal Hate Crimes Legislation? Stay Tuned.

Helen Zia

Helen Zia is a contributing editor to Ms., *a magazine that focuses on feminist issues, and is the author of* Asian American Dreams: The Emergence of an American People.

High profile attacks on women in recent years have prompted many Americans to view some violent acts against women to be motivated by hate and to propose expanding federal hate crimes legislation to include gender. Opponents argue that if gender is added to hate crime laws, most rapes and assaults against women would be prosecuted as hate crimes and would clog the criminal justice system with gender-bias cases. In reality, prosecutors would be required to present substantial evidence that a rape or assault was motivated by hate. Some victims of violent crime have been targeted simply because they were women, therefore hate crime laws prohibiting gender-motivated violence must be enacted.

Nine days before the United States Senate voted to include gender in federal hate crimes legislation in June 1999, a gang of men descended on scores of women in New York City's Central Park. Many of the women were sexually assaulted. Some were stripped of their clothes. Others were robbed. The attacks, which were caught on video by more than one amateur filmmaker, were by no means the most violent on that day in New York City, but they were certainly the most publicized.

And many of the women's rights activists who watched tapes of the attacks with horror were heartened to see that the response to the event seemed to represent a sea of change in how violence against women is viewed. There, for example, was civil rights activist Al Sharpton, standing at the scene of the crime, surrounded by victims, onlookers, and an ocean of television cameras, unexpectedly invoking the word "misogyny" to describe the climate that had given rise to these assaults.

Feminist activists can only hope that the Central Park attacks will trigger the same "click" for the U.S. House of Representatives as they apparently did for Sharpton and other men who seem to understand for the first time the danger that goes hand in hand with being female. The hate crimes amendment, which at press time was waiting to go into conference committee, is expected to meet tough opposition from House members. Indeed, the House may be a much harder sell than the Senate, where the amendment passed by a surprisingly wide margin of 57 to 42. Still, says Jacqueline Payne, policy attorney for National Organization of Women Legal Defense and Education Fund (NOW LDEF), which led the effort to include gender, "it seems unlikely that the amendment will pass into law this session." [The Senate supported the hate crimes amendment, while Congress opposed it in October 2000.]

Notable in the press coverage of the Senate's passage of the hate crimes bill was a curious underreporting of the bill's gender component. The *New York Times*, for example, trumpeted the headline SENATE EXPANDS HATE CRIMES LAW TO INCLUDE GAYS, disclosing six paragraphs into the story that the bill would also add handicapped status and "sex" to the categories covered.

While the press may have avoided the gender issue, the conference committees and the House of Representatives debating the legislation cannot. The question of whether violence against women is truly a hate crime must come up, just as it did in the many arguments that preceded the Senate vote. The feminists who brought the issue of gender-based hate crimes to the national policy arena not only ran into predictable political resistance but also encountered problems with the very framework of hate crimes law.

Gender-based violence

Consider the following scenario:

A white man works as a hotel maintenance worker in a secluded, mountainous area. Three people of color check into a room. He gets into their room on a ruse, ties them up, and assaults and kills them one by one. Emboldened by his act, he soon locates another person of color, then assaults and decapitates the victim. When the man is caught, he confesses that he has fantasized about killing people of color for 30 years. Could this be considered a hate crime?

Now substitute women for people of color in that scenario. Could *this* be considered a hate crime?

Most people can readily imagine the first example to be a hate crime. Strong and abhorrent images of bigotry based on race, religion, national origin, or sexual orientation have been etched in our minds: the enslavement of African Americans, the Holocaust against Jews, Jim Crow in the South, the internment of Japanese Americans, the Stonewall attack on gays.

Women are also the victims of horrific gender-based violence. For example, the scenario above really happened, in and near California's

Yosemite National Park in February 1999. The suspected killer admitted he had "fantasized about killing women for 30 years." Carole Carrington, mother of Carole Sund and grandmother of Juli Sund—two of the victims—testified before the House Judiciary Committee that the killings were hate crimes against women. "What else could they be?" she asked a group of reporters after her testimony. "A person who doesn't know the people at all and murders them only because they are women? It has to be that."

The religious right has worked to block hate crimes laws that include sexual orientation, but in fact, it's gender that has increasingly become a major sticking point. After the murder of Matthew Shepard, it even seemed that antigay conservatives would concede that gay men and lesbians could be targets of hate crimes. And indeed, a number of conservative senators did admit that it was time to address violence against gays with federal legislation. But making the federal legislative case for gender as a hate crime isn't as straightforward. Part of the problem has to do with how people think about rape—the quintessential crime against women. "Many people just don't believe that rapes happen because of hatred of women. It's like the old days of having to argue that domestic violence isn't a personal problem or a private matter," says NOW LDEF's Payne.

Perceptions and misperceptions of rape

Representatives from NOW LDEF and other organizations that took the cause to Congress found themselves caught between various perceptions and misperceptions about rape. Those who oppose including gender as a hate crime are using the feminists' own argument that "every rape is a hate crime" against women. Senator Orrin Hatch (R.-Utah), who repeatedly spoke against the bill on the Senate floor, reportedly argued in a subcommittee that including gender would turn "garden-variety rapes" into federal cases. He introduced a counter hate crimes bill that excluded gender, which was also approved by the Senate in June 2000, but only narrowly, in a 50 to 49 vote.

Many people just don't believe that rapes happen because of hatred of women.

Hatch isn't alone in his belief that men who commit "garden-variety rapes" shouldn't be charged with a federal offense. In initial discussions of hate crimes legislation, Patricia Reuss, senior policy analyst for NOW LDEF, found herself responding to the notion that the large number of rapes would bog down the federal government. When civil rights advocates gathered for an initial meeting at the U.S. Department of Justice, Reuss and her coalition were among the very few who advocated for the inclusion of gender in the hate crimes amendment. Agents from the FBI were saying, "But there are so many rapes and attempted rapes, the FBI can't look into all of them." Reuss responded: "Please forgive me that there are so many rapes. I'm sorry for all the rapes. But isn't that all the more reason to pursue gender-based crimes as hate crimes?"

The issue of "too many rapes" is a smoke screen. Under federal hate crimes law, not every rape would be pursued as a hate crime, in the same way that not every criminal act involving people of different races, religions, or national origins is pursued as a hate crime. Of the hundreds of thousands of crimes each year against property and persons that fall under various federally protected categories, the Department of Justice has selected only 36 hate crimes in the last five years to prosecute.

Under federal hate crimes law, not every rape would be pursued as a hate crime.

On this practical and legal level, it's simple to counter the argument that gender-based crimes would overwhelm the federal courts. Sexual assaults and other gender crimes would be evaluated in the same stringent manner as existing federal hate crimes. Before a hate crime moves into the federal realm, it is reviewed for certain criteria: epithets and bias language, extreme brutality that goes beyond "typical" violence, mutilation, patterns of behavior that might indicate a bias motive, and seemingly motiveless cruelty. Given these qualifications, the Central Park assaults, for example, would not be considered hate crimes. Cases that do meet these criteria undergo further screening to evaluate why the federal government should intervene in state crimes. Since sexual assault is a serious crime in every state, in theory rape victims should find justice at the local level, without federal intervention. In reality, that doesn't happen often enough. There are an estimated 300,000 rapes and sexual assaults reported each year. But in 1996, there were only 30,000 convictions for rape and sexual assault in state courts. (Statistics are not yet available for subsequent years.)

One major reason for federal intervention is the failure of local authorities to act appropriately, as in the case of a Florida judge who released an accused rapist, then chastised the victim for bringing the rape upon herself with the type of clothing she was wearing. And sometimes perpetrators are released because they are friends or family of police officers and politicians.

For crimes to come under federal hate crimes law, the U.S. attorney general must certify in writing that federal prosecution would be "in the public interest and necessary to secure substantial justice." But because so few crimes fall into this category, and with so few prosecutions brought on behalf of female hate crimes victims, it's absurd to think that the federal court system will be flooded with hate-rape prosecutions and irrational to conclude that the federal criminal justice process will change dramatically with the inclusion of gender in the law.

Still, the value of hate crimes legislation based on gender is twofold: it will inform the public about gender-based hate crimes; and local authorities will be kept honest because of the oversight of a higher power.

But the cultural opposition is still formidable. At congressional hearings and in policy briefings over the past decade, women's advocates have confronted the cultural notions surrounding rape—for example, that men rape women because of love, or at least lust, but not hate. Or that sexual assault is an "opportunity crime"—that a "normal" man will rape an "attractive" woman if he has an opportunity. This differs from the view of hate crimes, which are not seen as "normal" events. "Gender is treated as somehow different," says Payne.

On the cultural level, public opinion may need a paradigm shift for gender crimes to be seen as hate crimes—a shift on the magnitude of moving domestic violence out of the private realm into the public policy arena, a change that took three decades of constant effort by women activists. Or a shift like the one that saw date rape and marital rape treated as sexual violence. If there can be anything positive to come out of the Central Park assaults, it's that they may help to engender this shift.

"We're not creating new law—the changes are so minor," says Michael Lieberman, the Washington, D.C. counsel of the Anti-Defamation League, which developed model legislation for bias crimes. "But we are in the process of institutionalizing the concept that rape and gender-based crimes are hate crimes."

What remains to be done is to show how gender, like sexual orientation and race, fits the [hate crime] paradigm.

Women are not the only likely targets of hate crimes motivated by gender bias. As documented by the National Coalition of Anti-Violence Programs, transgendered male-to-females are frequent targets. But gathering data on transgendered violence is difficult, and the 1990 Hate Crimes Statistics Act, which established a federal data collection system based on the voluntary reports of local law enforcement agencies, does not identify hate crimes based on bias against transgendered people. Men who are perceived to be "too feminine" or women perceived to be "too masculine" have also long experienced bigotry, without civil rights recourse.

But women are the only group seeking hate crimes protection who don't constitute a minority. Though ignorance of a particular minority group has often been cited as a cause of hate-based violence, it's hard to argue that ignorance of women leads to bigotry, given that most people have had some contact with women. Shadowy, woman-hating cults exist, but no armed militia or ideology advocates the extermination of women. We can't, for example, point to hate groups like the Ku Klux Klan or Aryan Nations, which Buford Furrow belonged to when he shot up a Jewish community center in Los Angeles and murdered Filipino American Joseph Ileto. Rather, it's individuals, like the alleged killer of the women near Yosemite and Canadian Marc Lepine, who tend to commit hate crimes against women. In 1989, Lepine began a killing spree of 14 women by executing six engineering students at the University of Montreal while shouting, "You're all a bunch of feminists." This was clearly a gender-based hate crime.

Not so long ago, civil rights experts didn't include Asian Americans and Latinos under federal protections against racially motivated hate crimes. But the hate crimes paradigm shifted—as it also did when it was shown that people of color and other "targets" of hate could also commit crimes of bigotry. With the proliferation of hate groups all too willing to connect the dots between disenfranchised people, a deeper understanding of bias crimes has emerged. What remains to be done is to show how gender, like sexual orientation and race, fits the paradigm.

Gender crimes are hate crimes

Meanwhile, to help lawmakers discern between "garden-variety rapes" and gender-motivated hate crimes, NOW LDEF is building a list of cases that match criteria considered for current hate crimes categories. Among its cases are those involving severe circumstances, like the murders of the four women in and near Yosemite National Park. There are also those taken up by the Department of Justice because of underprosecution or misconduct by local authorities.

It will take continued vigilance and hard work to change the cultural perceptions of gender crimes as hate crimes. But the effort is worth it, because the fact that the federal government might intervene will motivate many local authorities to do a better job of prosecuting rape and other violent acts against women.

NOW LDEF's Payne encourages women to be visible in fighting hate crimes and to remind elected officials that gender-based crimes *are* hate crimes. "Some members of Congress say that hate crimes law is not an issue for women, that they don't hear from women," says Payne. "We know that's not true, but politicians need to feel the heat. Women need to name these crimes as hate crimes."

12

Most Crimes Against Women Are Not Hate Crimes

Cathy Young

Cathy Young is the vice president of the Women's Freedom Network and the author of Ceasefire: Why Women and Men Must Join Forces to Achieve True Equality.

Adding gender to the existing hate crime statute that includes race, religion, and ethnicity is not necessary. "Hate crimes" against women as vicious as the murders of African American James Byrd and gay college student Matthew Shepard are rare. Even among crimes motivated by hatred toward homosexuals, 80 percent of the victims are men. Enacting laws that prohibit gender-motivated violence against women is unjust because it ignores bias-motivated violence perpetrated by men against men. Moreover, the criteria for a crime to be a considered a gender-biased offense is loose enough to be applied to any case of rape or assault and would make many undeserving offenders vulnerable to federal prosecution. The call to classify crimes by gender is more of an effort to push political ideas than to protect victims or punish criminals.

The fatal beating of 21-year-old University of Wyoming student Matthew Shepard, apparently motivated at least in part by his homosexuality, has renewed the debate over hate crime legislation. The murder prompted calls from gay activists, editorial pages, and public officials, including Attorney General Janet Reno and President Clinton, for passage of the Federal Hate Crimes Protection Act. This bill would allow federal prosecution of crimes motivated by hatred based on gender, sexual orientation, and disability. [The bill did not pass.]

In their recent book *Hate Crimes: Criminal Law and Identity Politics*, criminologists James Jacobs and Kimberly Potter argue that ordinary criminal law provides adequate protection for victims of hate crimes—a point underscored by the Shepard case, in which prosecutors plan to seek the death penalty for the accused killers. Jacobs and Potter also warn that focusing on the identity aspects of crimes with often ambiguous motives can exacerbate tensions between groups, and they note that hate crime laws raise First Amendment concerns because they tend to punish perpetrators for their beliefs. But apart from the general problems posed by laws that single out "hate" or "bias" crimes, the bill before Congress contains an especially insidious provision: the addition of gender to the existing categories of race, religion, and ethnicity.

Gender-based hate crimes are uncommon

Except for one or two sensational cases, such as the 1989 massacre of 14 female engineering students at the University of Montreal by Marc Lepine, one would be hard pressed to think of a gender-based hate crime comparable to the murder of Shepard or of James Byrd, the black man dragged to his death behind a pickup truck in Texas last summer. Even anti-gay violence is directed at men more than 80 percent of the time.

But many feminists argue that we simply fail to recognize the gender bias in crimes against women such as rape ("both a symbol and an act of women's subordinate social status to men," according to University of Michigan law professor Catharine MacKinnon) and domestic abuse. These theories—distilled to sheer lunacy in the work of Andrea Dworkin, who believes that women live under "a police state where every man is deputized" and that heterosexual sex is a violation by definition—may be intellectually stimulating to some, but they are far too speculative to serve as a basis for legislation.

Forensic psychology does not support the view that rapists are driven primarily by hatred toward women rather than, say, sexual compulsion or anger at the whole world. The feminist interpretation of rape as intrinsically gender-motivated cannot explain sexual assaults on boys, or the fact that "date rape" is no less common among gay men than among heterosexuals. The statement that "women are raped because they are women" may ring true, but in a biological rather than a political sense: When a man's sexual urges are directed toward women, chances are that his sexual aggression will be too.

Domestic violence

As for domestic violence, University of British Columbia psychologist Donald Dutton and other researchers have found that wife beating is far more strongly associated with "borderline personality disorder" (characterized by a proclivity for intense relationships, insecurity, and rage) than with patriarchal attitudes; drugs and alcohol are major factors as well. Aside from the much-debated issue of female aggression toward male partners, it is no longer in dispute that physical abuse is at least as common in gay and lesbian couples as in heterosexual ones.

One might point out, too, that male violence is directed mainly at other males. If sexual assault and intimate violence against women are related to gender, surely so are male-on-male attacks triggered by real or perceived slights, sexual rivalry, and thrill seeking. Thugs who rape a woman may also beat up men just for fun, like the teenagers convicted in the notorious 1989 rape of the Central Park jogger. Describing their "wilding" rampage in the park to a detective, one of the teens said that "wilding" meant "going around, punching, hitting on people"—not just women. Yet the attack on the jogger became a paradigm of gender-motivated violence to many feminists; it was cited as such by Helen Neuborne, then president of the National Organization for Women Legal Defense Fund, in testimony to the Senate Judiciary Committee.

Forensic psychology does not support the view that rapists are driven primarily by hatred toward women rather than, say, sexual compulsion or anger at the whole world.

Despite these logical flaws, the radical feminist theory of "gender violence" has made significant inroads in the legal system. It was incorporated into the Violence Against Women Act (VAWA), passed by Congress in 1994, which allows federal civil rights suits for violent crimes "motivated by gender." The application of VAWA, however, is limited by the fact that it provides only for monetary damages. Such litigation, usually lengthy, doesn't make sense unless there are significant assets to go after. Some VAWA cases involve divorcing wives alleging abuse by wealthy husbands; recently, a VAWA lawsuit was filed against basketball bad boy Dennis Rodman by a Las Vegas Hilton casino employee who accuses him of grabbing her by the sides of the torso and lifting her (which, she claims, caused her underwire bra to be painfully pushed into her breast). Other legal action has targeted deep-pocket entities: A suit filed in December 1995 by Christine Brzonkala, a former Virginia Polytechnic student who claimed that she was raped by two male students, named not only the alleged perpetrators but the college as defendants.

Double jeopardy

The Federal Hate Crimes Protection Act, by contrast, would open the door to federal criminal prosecutions for sexual assault or domestic violence, particularly in high-profile cases where an acquittal or dismissal in state courts results in an outcry from women's groups. Men accused of these crimes would effectively lose their double jeopardy protections, like the Los Angeles policemen who were convicted of beating Rodney King. (Under the doctrine of "dual sovereignty," a federal offense is not the same as a state offense, even if it consists of the same action.) However gratifying the outcome of some cases might be, the process is troubling. Moreover, in a "bias" case, the defendant could find himself on trial for having sexist views, watching X-rated movies, or mistreating other women, even if they never went to the police.

Testifying in favor of the expanded federal law last June, Assistant Attorney General Eric Holder reassured the Senate Judiciary Committee that very few "gender-motivated hate crimes" could be prosecuted in federal court, since such prosecutions would require proof of "gender-based bias." But judging from the history of VAWA litigation, which he invoked as a model, the criteria would be elastic enough to apply to any claim of rape or abuse. And that is clearly what the advocates want. At a symposium on VAWA in May 1999, NOW Legal Defense Fund attorney Julie Goldscheid praised the courts for recognizing, "in language that is really heartening to a women's rights advocate, that domestic violence and sexual assault are gender-motivated crimes rooted in the history of discrimination against women."

In Christine Brzonkala's suit against Virginia Polytechnic, the courts found evidence of bias in the fact that the two alleged rapists were virtual strangers to the plaintiff (which should rattle feminist activists who have denounced the notion that acquaintance rape is a lesser crime); that the attack had no motive other than rape; and that, according to Brzonkala, one of the defendants told her, "You'd better not have any fucking diseases." It is worth noting that after hearing the evidence, a Virginia grand jury refused to indict the two men, who claimed that they had consensual sex with Brzonkala—which did not keep her from being invited to the White House Conference on Hate Crimes as a spokeswoman for hate crime victims.

Wife beating is far more strongly associated with "borderline personality disorder". . . than with patriarchal attitudes.

In other cases, federal courts have ruled that alleged acts of sexual violence by themselves justify a claim of gender motivation. In *Jane Doe v. The Rev. Gerald Hartz,* a 1997 case in which an Iowa woman accused her parish priest of kissing and groping her, the court specifically stated that unwanted sexual advances met the gender motivation requirement even if they were "intended to satisfy the actor's sexual desires," since they could also "be demeaning and belittling, and may reasonably be inferred to be intended to have that purpose or to relegate another to an inferior status." In other words, if a priest makes unwanted sexual advances toward a young man, his goal is merely to satisfy his lust, but if he makes unwanted sexual advances toward a young woman, his goal is to relegate her to inferior status. The suit was later thrown out on the grounds that the alleged conduct didn't rise to the level of a violent crime as required by VAWA, but the lower court's interpretation of gender bias went unchallenged.

Two federal courts have given a green light to civil rights suits under VAWA based on allegations of spousal abuse. One case is pending, while the other was settled during the appeals process. Meanwhile, courts in some of the 17 states with hate crime laws that cover gender have applied those statutes in cases of spousal assault. In 1993, a New Hampshire judge used that state's hate crime law in sentencing a man convicted of misdemeanor assault on his girl-friend, after four other women testified that he had abused them while they dated and harassed them after their breakups. There were no allegations that the defendant had ever assaulted any women with whom he was not intimately involved. Such an approach contrasts sharply with the usual analysis of "hate crimes" based on race or ethnicity, where the fact that the victim is selected at random, on the basis of group membership rather than a personal relationship, is considered indicative of bias.

Many advocates of hate crime laws are less concerned with protecting victims or even punishing offenders than with making a political point about the pervasiveness of bigotry in American life. Still, most acts classified as hate crimes probably are based at least partly on actual bigotry. In the case of gender, not only the special treatment of hate crimes but the use of the hate-crime label itself—and the analogy with crimes motivated by racial, ethnic, or anti-gay bias—is part of an ideological agenda. The goal is not only to affirm that violence against women is a matter of special concern but that it's part of a male war against women. If no one challenges such ideas in the political arena, it's likely that legislators and judges will continue to give them a seal of approval.

Organizations to Contact

The editors have compiled the following list of organizations concerned with the issues debated in this book. The descriptions are derived from materials provided by the organizations. All have publications or information available for interested readers. The list was compiled on the date of publication of the present volume; the information provided here may change. Be aware that many organizations take several weeks or longer to respond to inquiries, so allow as much time as possible.

American Civil Liberties Union (ACLU)
132 W. 43rd St., New York, NY 10036
(212) 944-9800 • fax: (212) 869-9065
e-mail: aclu@aclu.org • website: www.aclu.org

The ACLU is a national organization that works to defend Americans' civil rights guaranteed in the U.S. Constitution. It publishes the semiannual newsletter *Civil Liberties Alert* as well as the briefing papers "Hate Speech on Campus" and "Racial Justice."

Anti-Defamation League (ADL)
823 United Nations Plaza, New York, NY 10017
(212) 490-2525
website: www.adl.org

The ADL is an international organization that fights prejudice and extremism. It collects, organizes, and distributes information about anti-Semitism, hate crimes, bigotry, and racism, and also monitors hate groups and extremists on the Internet. Among its many publications are the reports *Explosion of Hate: The Growing Danger of the National Alliance*, *Danger: Extremism—The Major Vehicles and Voices on America's Far Right Fringe*, and *Hate on the World Wide Web*.

Aryan Nations
Church of Jesus Christ Christian, PO Box 362, Hayden Lake, ID 83835
e-mail: aryannhq@nidlink.com • website: www.christian-aryannations.com

Aryan Nations promotes racial purity and believes that whites are persecuted by Jews and blacks. It publishes the *Aryan Nations Newsletter* and pamphlets such as *New World Order in North America*, *Aryan Warriors Stand*, and *Know Your Enemies*.

Canadian Centre on Racism and Prejudice
Box 505, Station Desjardins, Montreal, QC H5B 1B6 Canada
(514) 727-2936

Affiliated with the Center for Democratic Renewal in Atlanta, Georgia, the Canadian center monitors the activities of white supremacist groups and the development of the far right in Canada. It publishes the bimonthly newsletter *Bulletin*.

Center for Democratic Renewal (CDR)
PO Box 50469, Atlanta, GA 30302
(404) 221-0025 • fax: (404) 221-0045
e-mail: Info@thecdr.org • website: www.thecrd.org

Formerly known as the National Anti-Klan Network, this nonprofit organization monitors hate group and white supremacist activity in America and opposes bias-motivated violence. It publishes the bimonthly *Monitor* magazine, the report *The Fourth Wave: A Continuing Conspiracy to Burn Black Churches*, and the book *When Hate Groups Come to Town*.

Center for the Study of Hate and Extremism
Department of Criminal Justice, College of Social and Behavioral Sciences
California State University, San Bernardino
5500 University Pkwy., San Bernardino, CA 92407
email: blevin8@aol.com • website: www.hatemonitor.org

The Center for the Study of Hate and Extremism is a nonpartisan research and policy center that investigates the ways that bigotry, extremism, and terrorism deny civil or human rights to people on the basis of race, ethnicity, religion, gender, sexual orientation, disability or other relevant status characteristics. The center seeks to aid scholars, community activists, government officials, law enforcement, the media and others with objective information to aid them in their examination and implementation of law and policy.

Euro-American Alliance
PO Box 2-1776, Milwaukee, WI 53221
(414) 423-0565

This organization opposes racial mixing and advocates self-segregation for whites. It publishes a number of pamphlets, including *Who Hates Whom?* and *Who We Really Are*.

Human Rights and Race Relations Centre
120 Eglinton Dr. East, Suite 500, Toronto, ON M4P 1E2, Canada
(416) 481-7793

The center is a charitable organization that opposes all types of discrimination. Its goal is to develop a society free of racism, in which each ethnic group respects the rights of other groups. It recognizes individuals and institutions that excel in the promotion of race relations or work for the elimination of discrimination. The center publishes the weekly newspaper *New Canada*.

Human Rights Campaign (HRC)
919 18th St. NW, Washington, DC 20006
(202) 628-4160 • fax: (202) 347-5323
email: hrc@hrc.org • website: www.hrc.org

Founded in 1980, the HRC is the largest gay and lesbian political organization. This organization seeks to protect the civil rights of gay, lesbian, bisexual, and transgendered Americans. It lobbies the federal government on gay, lesbian, and AIDS issues, fights discriminatory legislation, and supports the Employment Non-Discrimination Act (ENDA), a bill that would protect Americans from being terminated from their jobs on grounds of sexual orientation. The HRC also sponsors the National Coming Out Project.

League for Human Rights of B'nai B'rith Canada
15 Hove St., Downsview, ON M3H 4Y8 Canada
(416) 633-6227

Affiliated with the U.S. Anti-Defamation League, this organization works to end the defamation of Jews and to ensure fair treatment for all Canadian citizens. It publishes the annual *Review of Anti-Semitism in Canada.*

National Alliance
PO Box 90, Hillsboro, WV 24946
(304) 653-4600
website: www.natvan.com

The alliance believes that the white race is superior to all other races in intelligence, ability, and creativity. It argues that it is the obligation of all whites to fight for the creation of a white nation that is free of non-Aryan influence. It publishes the newsletter *Free Speech* and the magazine *National Vanguard.*

National Association for the Advancement of Colored People (NAACP)
4805 Mt. Hope Dr., Baltimore, MD 21215-3297
(410) 358-8900 • fax: (410) 486-9255 • hotline: (410) 521-4939
website: www.naacp.org

The NAACP is the oldest and largest civil rights organization in the United States. Its principal objective is to ensure the political, educational, social, and economic equality of minorities. It publishes the magazine *Crisis* ten times a year as well as a variety of newsletters, books, and pamphlets.

National Coalition Against Censorship
275 Seventh Ave., New York, NY 10001
(212) 807-6222 • fax: (212) 807-6245
e-mail: ncac@ncac.org • website: www.ncac.org

The coalition represents more than forty national organizations that work to prevent suppression of free speech and the press. It publishes the quarterly *Censorship News.*

National Gay and Lesbian Task Force (NGLTF)
1700 Kalorama Rd. NW, Washington, DC 20009-2624
(202) 332-6483 • fax: (202) 332-0207
e-mail: ngltf@ngltf.org • website: www.ngltf.org

NGLTF is a civil rights organization that fights bigotry and violence against gays and lesbians. It sponsors conferences and organizes local groups to promote civil rights legislation for gays and lesbians. It publishes the monthly *Eye on Equality* column and distributes reports, fact sheets, and bibliographies on antigay violence.

People for the American Way Foundation
2000 M St. NW, Suite 400, Washington, DC 20036
(800) 326-7329
e-mail: pfaw@pfaw.org • website: www.pfaw.org

People for the American Way Foundation opposes the political agenda of the religious right. Through public education, lobbying, and legal advocacy, the foundation works to defend equal rights. The foundation publishes *Hostile Climate*, a report detailing intolerant incidents directed against gays and lesbians, and organizes the Students Talk About Race (STAR) program, which trains college students to lead high school discussions on intergroup relations.

Southern Poverty Law Center (SPLC)
400 Washington Ave., Montgomery, AL 36104
(334) 264-0286
website: www.splcenter.org

The center litigates civil cases to protect the rights of poor people, particularly when those rights are threatened by white supremacist groups. The affiliated Klanwatch Project and the Militia Task Force collect data on white supremacist groups and militias and promote the adoption and enforcement by states of antiparamilitary training laws. The center publishes the monthly *Klanwatch Intelligence Report*, and the reports *Responding to Hate at School*, and *Ten Ways to Fight Hate*.

Stormfront
PO Box 6637, West Palm Beach, FL 33405
(561) 833-0030 • fax: (561) 820-0051
e-mail: comments@stormfront.org • website: www.stormfront.org

Stormfront is dedicated to preserving "white western culture, ideals, and freedom of speech." It serves as a resource for white political and social action groups. It publishes the weekly newsletter *Stormwatch*, and its website contains articles and position papers such as *White Nationalism: Key Concepts* and *Equality: Man's Most Dangerous Myth*.

White Aryan Resistance (WAR)
PO Box 65, Fallbrook, CA 92088
(760) 723-8996
e-mail: warmetzger@aol.com • website: www.resist.com

WAR believes the white race is in danger of extinction and advocates for a separatist state for whites only. It publishes the monthly newspaper *WAR*, produces the *Race and Reason* television show, distributes "white power" music recordings, and maintains a racial news and information hotline.

World Church of the Creator (WCOTC)
PO Box 2002, East Peoria, IL 61611
(309) 699-0135
e-mail: PMHale1@aol.com • website: www.creator.org

WCOTC is a religion that is based on love for the white race above all others. Its goal is to ensure the expansion and advancement of the white race and believes that nature's highest law requires each species to fight for its own survival. It publishes *Nature's Eternal Religion*, *The White Man's Bible*, and the monthly publication *The Struggle*.

Bibliography

Books

Donald Altshiller — *Hate Crimes: A Reference Handbook*. Santa Barbara, CA: ABC-CLIO, 1999.

Benjamin Bowling — *Violent Racism: Victimization, Policing, and Social Context*. New York: Oxford University Press, 1998.

Howard L. Bushart, John R. Craig, and Myra Barnes — *Soldiers of God: White Supremacists and Their Holy War for America*. New York: Kensington, 1998.

Judith Butler — *Excitable Speech: A Politics of the Performative*. New York: Routledge, 1997.

Richard Delgado and Jean Stefancic — *Must We Defend Nazis? Hate Speech, Pornography, and the First Amendment*. New York: New York University Press, 1997.

John D'Emilio, William B. Turner, and Urvashi Vaid — *Creating Change: Sexuality, Public Policy, and Civil Rights*. New York: St. Martin's Press, 2000.

James B. Jacobs and Kimberly Potter — *Hate Crimes: Criminal Law and Identity Politics*. New York: New York University Press, 1998.

Jeffrey Kaplan and Tore Bjorgo — *Nation and Race: The Developing Euro-American Racist Subculture*. Boston, MA: Northeastern University Press, 1998.

Robert J. Kelly and Jess Maghan, eds. — *Hate Crime: The Global Politics of Polarization*. Carbondale: Southern Illinois University Press, 1998.

Alan Charles Kors and Harvey A. Silverglate — *The Shadow University*. New York: Free Press, 1998.

Alex Kotlowitz — *The Other Side of the River: A Story of Two Towns, a Death, and America's Dilemma*. New York: Doubleday, 1998.

Fredrick M. Lawrence — *Punishing Hate: Bias Crimes Under American Law*. Cambridge, MA: Harvard University Press, 1999.

LegiSchool Project — *Hate Behavior and Hate Crimes: What Motivates People to Hate? How Can We Prevent Hate Crimes in Our Schools and Communities?* Sacramento, CA: Senate Publications, 2000.

Barbara Perry — *In the Name of Hate: Understanding Hate Crimes*. New York: Routledge, 2000.

John W. Phillips — *Sign of the Cross: The Prosecutor's True Story of a Landmark Trial Against the Clan*. Louisville, KY: Westminster John Knox Press, 2000.

| Timothy C. Shiell | *Campus Hate Speech on Trial.* Lawrence: University Press of Kansas, 1999. |

Steven H. Shiffrin — *Dissent, Injustice, and the Meaning of America.* Princeton, NJ: Princeton University Press, 1999.

Philippa Strum — *When the Nazis Came to Skokie.* Lawrence: University Press of Kansas, 1999.

James Weinstein — *Hate Speech, Pornography, and the Radical Attack on Free Speech.* Boulder, CO: Westview 1999.

Martha T. Zingo — *Sex/Gender Outsiders, Hate Speech, and the Freedom of Expression.* Westport, CT: Praeger, 1998.

Periodicals

Richard D. Barton — "A Free Nation Can Overcome Forces of Hate," *San Diego Union-Tribune*, August 15, 1999. Available from 350 Camino de la Reina, San Diego, CA 92108-3003.

Robert O. Blanchard — "The 'Hate State' Myth," *Reason*, May 1999.

Lynette Clemetson — "The New Victims of Hate," *Newsweek*, November 6, 2000.

Adam Clymer — "Senate Expands Hate Crime Laws to Include Gays," *The New York Times*, June 21, 2000.

David Cullen — "Bullies in the Pulpit," *In These Times*, November 29, 1998.

Morris Dees — "Hate Crimes," *Vital Speeches of the Day*, February 1, 2000.

Mark Fritz — "Hate Crimes Hard to Track as Some Areas Report None," *Los Angeles Times*, August 23, 1999. Available from Reprints, Times Mirror Square, Los Angeles, CA 90053 or www.latimes.com.

Brendan Lemon — "The State of Hate," *Advocate*, April 13, 1999.

Brian Levin and Bruce Fein — "Does America Need a Federal Hate Crime Law?" *Insight on the News*, November 23, 1998. Available from 3600 New York Ave. NE, Washington, DC 20002.

Robert Stacy McCain — "Hate Crimes Not Big Problem in Race Relations," *Washington Times*, June 1, 1999. Available from 3600 New York Ave. NE, Washington, DC 20002.

Sarah J. McCarthy — "Fertile Ground for Terrorists?" *Humanist*, January/February 1999. Available from 1777 T St. NW, Washington, DC 20009-3175.

Terence Monmaney — "Reviving a Resort's Racial Pain," *Los Angeles Times*, January 18, 2001.

Lowell Ponte — "The Secret Hate in 'Hate Crimes,'" *Ideas on Liberty*, February 2001. Available from the Foundation for Economic Education, 30 S. Broadway, Irvington, NY 10533.

Deb Price — "We Need More Federal Involvement in Prosecuting Hate Crimes," *Liberal Opinion Week*, March 29, 1999. Available from PO Box 880, Vinton, IA 52349.

Maria Purdy — "Hate Crime Horror Stories," *'Teen*, March 2000.

Patrick Rogers — "Spurred to Action," *People Weekly*, December 11, 2000.

Jocelyn Y. Stewart — "Lest Hate Victim Be Forgotten," *Los Angeles Times*, January 25, 2001.

Guy Trebay — "Overkill: The Grand Guignol Murder of a Gay Man in Virginia," *Village Voice*, April 13, 1999. Available from 36 Cooper Square, New York, NY 10003.

Daniel E. Troy — "Hate Crime Laws Make Some More Equal than Others," *Wall Street Journal*, October 19, 1998.

Daniel E. Troy — "The GOP's Hearing Loss," *American Spectator*, November 1999.

Index